Hidden Miracles at
All Souls

Hidden Miracles at
All Souls

MARY ENDERSBEE

Photographs on cover and inside cover
by François Prins.

LAKELAND, Marshall, Morgan & Scott. A member of the Pentos
group, 1 Bath Street, London EC1V 9LB. Copyright © The
Parochial Church Council of All Souls Church, Langham Place,
1977. First published 1977. ISBN 0 551 00768 0. All rights reserved.
No part of this publication may be reproduced, stored in a retrieval
system, or transmitted, in any form or by any means, electronic,
mechanical, photocopying, recording or otherwise, without the
prior permission of the Copyright owner. Printed in Great Britain
by Hunt Barnard Printing Ltd., Aylesbury, Bucks.

CONTENTS

INTRODUCTION

What is All Souls?

The London tourist finds himself directed to notice briefly All Souls Church, the historic Anglican church 'with an unusual fluted spire', situated within sight of Oxford Circus tube station and next door to Broadcasting House in Langham Place.

The architectural guidebooks are more expansive, describing the building as the only remaining example of a galleried square 'Commissioners' Church' designed and built in 1824 by the famous Regency architect, John Nash, the inspiration behind the wide sweeping thoroughfare of Regent Street and Portland Place in London's West End. Indeed, most of them go on to explain that because the latter highway had to lie further east than intended, all Nash's ingenuity was required to put matters right. His solution was to place his new church, All Souls, at an angle on the south-east corner of Portland Place, the main body of it out of sight when viewed from the south and its circular portico, peristyle and spire, closing the vista.

But this advice and information tells not the half of the story of All Souls. Look at the outside of the church and there is little evidence of the incredible changes that have taken place within its walls. Furthermore, in God's economy, people matter more than buildings. The church in Langham Place is, in reality, a family of believing, worshipping Christians led by their Rector, the Rev. Michael Baughen, without whose enthusiasm and vision, this new era at the church would have been impossible.

Under his leadership the church, aware of its uniquely strategic position in the heart of London's shoppers' golden mile, seeks to minister to the varied parish needs and to the neighbourhood. To this end, there is a full time chaplain to five of the Oxford Street department stores, and weekly lunch-hour services, to reach out to the hundreds of shop and office workers in the vicinity, are held.

On the church's doorstep are the Central London Poly-technic in Upper Regent Street and the British Broadcasting Corporation. The church provides a full-time chaplain for the former and for the latter, a home for the BBC's Daily Service plus regular broadcasts by the congregation on the BBC World Service.

Meanwhile in the north-east residential corner of the parish, a Christian community centre for local residents of all ages is operated at the All Souls Clubhouse.

Because of its large student membership the church has also three lay pastors to care for the needs of these. With many big London hospitals not too far distant, medics, nurses and para-medical workers in training find a warm welcome too.

The family at All Souls is not allowed to be inward-looking. It supports thirty missionaries for a start! It has strong international links and at every service there are Christians present from all over the English-speaking world and beyond. Many are regular members, attracted at first by the warm descriptions of its ministry they have heard back home. Having come as visitors, they prefer to stay and become part of the family. Others come because they have heard the rector emeritus, the Rev. John Stott, preaching or lecturing on one of his many overseas tours. His name, more than any other, has given the church its international fol-lowing.

It is true also that his Christian character and logical expository preaching, during his twenty-five years as rector, have helped to make All Souls what it is today – 'the evan-gelical Anglican cathedral of the south east' as some call it.

However, when John Stott became rector in 1950, the church was already well known for its evangelical position, under the godly direction of his predecessor, the Rev. Harold Earnshaw-Smith. Before that it had varied in churchmanship, but always remained a well-attended and fashionable London landmark, with the famous Victorian Queen's Hall on its southern flank and, in 1932, dwarfed on the northern side by the tall jutting frontage of Broadcasting House, the full value of this latter proximity being realised when the BBC's religious department decided in 1951 that broadcasting the Daily Service from the studio-cum-chapel in the BBC building left a lot to be desired.

The re-opened and refurbished All Souls is still used to broadcast the fifteen-minute Daily Service, but within its 150-year-old exterior there is a new buzz of activity all day long. Seldom is the building empty, for its new facilities, when not being used by the church, are let to other organisations.

Normally the church family are in residence. On Sundays the 1,000-plus congregation, seated far more comfortably than ever before, can see the clergy and preacher in the chancel without difficulty. Coffee and meals are served afterwards in the new basement hall and refectory. On week-nights various groups meet in its relaxed surroundings: the International Fellowship, the Prayer Gathering, Fellowship Groups, Nursery Classes (for new Christians), Midweek, West One (groups who meet for relaxation and inspiration) and Core Year (a training programme for those who wish to be involved in the church's work and witness). The list is endless because often two activities are going on at the same time! All Souls may be a big church, with some 700 or more on its membership list, but every opportunity to relate to one another in smaller groups is taken and made much easier by the new building.

Yet in 1971, barely five years earlier, all this appeared a sheer impossibility. This book is a record of the impossible made possible by God in many incredible and exciting ways. The 'hidden miracles' of the title do not refer to the arches and foundations alone. Everyone who was involved in the building project discovered a new power to give and give again – and many are the stories of personal miracles of loving sacrifice that could be told.

This book is dedicated with love and gratitude to my fellow members of the church who have helped me tell this story. In particular my thanks are due to John Stott, David Trapnell and Michael Baughen for their invaluable advice and inspired leadership which enabled us all to see that the God of Abraham, the God of Moses, is the God whom we serve today.

Mary Endersbee

1   'Bomb All Souls!'

Rector says, 'Bomb All Souls for new church.'

Daily Telegraph

'A suggestion that historic All Souls Church, Langham Place, in the shadow of the BBC, should be "bombed" and a new one built was made in Australia yesterday by the Rev. John Stott, the Rector, when he was speaking in Perth during a lecture tour.

' "There would be a terrible public outcry if the building went," Mr Stott said. "But the Church cannot be hamstrung for every old building. I would like to sell the English Cathedrals to the National Trust, or keep the structures and radically change the insides . . . " '

When the above words appeared under the headline 'Rector says "Bomb All Souls for new church" ', in the *Daily Telegraph* for 4 February 1971, it created something of a minor sensation. For few people outside a tiny circle of John Stott's colleagues and advisers had any inkling of his attempts to free All Souls from the crippling frustrations under which it was working.

But for no one could the newspaper report have been more startling than for the brand new vicar, the Rev. Michael Baughen, who had just taken over the leadership of the church. He had been told by John Stott in December 1970, some six weeks before he left, that the tentative plans to alter the church were completely hush-hush. Now John

11

appeared to have let the cat out of the bag with a vengeance. There was no way that Michael Baughen could prevent the church's redevelopment from becoming a matter of public debate, and he was delighted to have it out in the open. It could now become a matter for prayer for the whole church family.

Asked for his immediate reactions to his colleague's statement, by Edmund Townsend of the *Daily Telegraph*, Michael Baughen gave his explanation of the situation facing the church: 'We are stuck in the middle of London and have no room for our different activities. We have to have meetings in rooms and halls scattered around the area. We cannot work in the way we want . . . We have no proper facilities.'

He went on, 'The real question is, "What do we do? Are we going to be custodians of a monument or are we going to face the challenge of the twentieth century?" '

The press report undoubtedly caused a stir. Peter Simple made lighthearted use of it in his *Daily Telegraph* 'Way of the World' column the next day, and Geoffrey Fletcher, the artist whose delicate line drawings of historic architectural gems often enhanced the pages of the same paper, wrote to Michael Baughen expressing his deep concern that the distinctively Nash church was in danger of being demolished, and enclosing a copy of his own sketch of the building made some years previously.

More significantly still, Michael received phone calls and letters from a number of property and finance companies eager to develop the church's strategic West End site, near to Oxford Street and Regent Street. The general idea was that the church could sell out completely and acquire another plot of land and rebuild, or keep the site but have a totally new building on it which would incorporate all the features necessary to maintain, if not enhance, the church's witness.

For John Stott, meanwhile, on his way home after six weeks in Australia, the unexpected press reaction to his 'off the cuff' remarks appeared surprising but providential. On his last day in Western Australia, spent in Perth, his host, the Archbishop, kindly allowed his sitting-room to be used for a press conference attended by four journalists. One was a young girl, keen to know how the church could be dragged into the twentieth century.

In his reply John Stott explained his own longing to see radicalism and conservatism in the church rightly balanced. But sometimes conservatism won the day – hampering a church's attempt to make radical changes. Take All Souls, for example. And with recent bombings and hijackings by Palestinian guerillas in mind, he added that in order to free the building for essential redevelopment, he found himself devoutly hoping and praying that All Souls would be bombed.

That night he flew to Hong Kong and was startled to find the tarmac buzzing with newsmen all wanting to know why he wanted to bomb All Souls. The young Australian reporter had sold the story to Reuters and an alert *Daily Telegraph* newsman had followed it up in London.

But what appeared news to many was in fact old history to others. For some two or three years previously, John Stott, with the help of four or five friends, had been trying very cautiously and correctly to probe around the sensitive area of the possible redevelopment of the church building, which was proving more and more of a financial and physical burden to its overflowing congregation, swelled in term time by students and in the summer by many visitors from abroad.

Back in 1968 the need for improved facilities had taxed the Parochial Church Council, a body of twenty-five to thirty men and women elected annually to have oversight of the church's finance and management. The lack of a church hall was self-evident, especially on Sundays when as few as fifty visitors to a buffet lunch could scarcely crowd down unattractive stone stairs and into the small lower room of the triangular-shaped building attached to the rear of the church, known as Church House.

(When All Souls Church opened in 1824 to serve the new parish carved out with three others from the parish of St Marylebone, it was not given the benefit of a parish hall. The problems this caused over the intervening 150 years are many and various.)

Another major item demanding the Council's attention was the organ, a particularly fine Willis instrument installed in 1951 and beginning to show definite signs of wear and tear. However, by July 1969 when the council looked afresh at the need for new facilities, they had decided to keep the organ going for a further five years in case major redevelopments took place. Increasing demands were also being made on the church's not very versatile Victorian interior; fixed pews and choir stalls made it impossible to meet socially within its walls in comfort. The pulpit set high up a winding stair to the right was visible to only a limited number of the congregation. In fact, little that took place in the sanctuary could be seen by those who were not sitting in the front rows of the gallery or the two centre blocks of pews. The view from the two side aisles was made even more difficult by Nash's large pillars and the Victorian front-facing fixed pews.

Another thought which occupied the minds of John Stott and his council at this time was how to face the challenge of the future. The sixties had brought such a wind of change in so many attitudes that the Church's old-fashioned language and liturgy was losing its allure. Its antiquated buildings were not helping either. How could the present All Souls meet the challenge of the year 2000? What facilities should the church provide? A redevelopment committee was appointed that July to look at just this kind of question. It consisted of John Stott, Ted Schroder (a curate at All Souls), David Trapnell and George Cansdale (church-wardens), Eric Starling (an architect) and Robert Howarth (a lay member of staff working among overseas visitors to the church).

But in September when the council met for its annual day conference outside London to discuss these matters at greater length, they discovered it was not the only radical change afoot. A memo from John Stott proposed an unprecedented alteration in the staff structure. He wished the church to have better pastoral oversight, and had sought the Bishop of London's approval in general for his desire to invite a man to become vicar: a senior pastor to take over the leadership of the church and relieve him of much of his pastoral duties. This would free him to accept the many invitations he was receiving to preach and teach – especially overseas – while retaining his strong links with All Souls, where he had been rector for nineteen, and curate for five years.

Despite this new suggestion, John Stott turned the council's attention again to more pressing long-term needs. Pointing out the hopeless inadequacy of the present buildings and the fact that the church could not afford to maintain them, he proposed that 'we ought to develop our All Souls site in an imaginative and financially viable way and give a lead to other churches in urban areas which are considering redevelopment'. On the negative side he added that 'as yet, no nationally known architect had been found who was willing to associate himself with the project'.

With the news of a possible new incumbent, all thoughts of adapting buildings switched temporarily to the rectory in Weymouth Street and the provision of accommodation for the vicar, especially if he were married with a family. Plans and negotiations were put in hand to enable John Stott and the students who shared the rectory, to move out and for the rector, the mews house behind was to be demolished and rebuilt. Meanwhile the search continued for a suitable architect to help develop the church.

But, as fast as negotiations with the new incumbent reached a satisfactory conclusion in early 1970, the floating of the idea of redeveloping All Souls ground slowly to a halt, floundering on the mudflats of architectural disapproval from a man who was considered to be a Nash expert. He reacted very unfavourably to any idea of changing All Souls, even if the distinctive steeple and rotunda were left intact. It was a plan liable to bring the wrath of many on the architect's head, he said. It would be a bold man who would risk his reputation meddling with such a historic building.

So in May 1970 when the appointment of the new vicar was announced – the Rev. Michael Baughen, who would arrive in December, having just relinquished his work at Holy Trinity, Platt Fields, Manchester – John Stott and the council decided with mixed feelings to shelve any plans for redevelopment – for the moment.

Michael Baughen knew all about these shelved plans when he arrived at All Souls, but his chief concern was a pastoral one, and it was no sinecure. For a start, his change of role was a big one from rector of a friendly close-knit community parish in the north to a sprawling business, flat and bed-sit-land parish in impersonal central London, with a congregation that lived to a large extent outside its boundaries. Furthermore, he was pioneering a new role in All Souls itself, with the much-loved and respected figure of John Stott still on the staff, and five curates and one parish worker as his team.

Over and above all the upheavals of his arrival at All Souls, Michael Baughen held very strongly to his original brief: to be a pastor to the whole flock, young and old. He wanted most of all to encourage the church to feel like a family that not only worshipped together on Sundays, but also prayed and stayed together during the course of the week in between.

To do this it was essential that all members of all ages could meet together – and from the start, that proved difficult. On Sundays in the services 500 regulars were lost among the 500 visitors. So the family 'feel' was hard to create there. Any attempt to gather after services was also thwarted by the lack of a building large enough to relax in.

More personally the proof of this problem came home, literally, when Michael and Myrtle Baughen opened the rectory on Sunday evenings for fellowship, inviting the church family back after the service for a relaxed time of hymn singing, coffee and discussion. After a few months, the big L-shaped sitting-room was bursting its seams, even with the door off its hinges, as more and more people took up their invitation. Where else could this Sunday night gathering be held? No room in Church House was adequate, so in desperation the group was split in two – one upstairs and one downstairs as second best.

On week nights the various sections of the congregation met separately, but, once a fortnight, the Waldegrave Hall in Duke Street tried to accommodate everyone for the prayer meeting. At least here was one opportunity to be together as a family for prayer and fellowship!

But the family was not at the prayer meeting. It was not nearly as well attended as it should be. In the early months of 1971 Michael Baughen's conviction grew that if he was to stay at All Souls at all, God would have to unite the scattered membership through the prayer meeting, strengthening the bonds of love and friendship, so that – most important of all – the time of prayer became central to the church's life and was not attended just by a faithful minority.

The lack of suitable buildings struck him also when looking at the church's evangelism. In its outreach Michael felt the buildings hampered rather than helped. After services there was nowhere to encourage enquirers to stay and talk quietly in comfort. On week nights, anyone coming to the church for counsel or help would find the building closed as the congregation met elsewhere.

To John Stott in particular the closed church was a grievous mistake. It was a monstrous waste of money, in his view, to have a church used a few hours a week only on Sundays. With the ever increasing need for homes and houses, an empty unused church was a poor witness to those around.

Set against all this concern was the definite proposition put to the church by a development company in the City of London as soon as a hint of possible redevelopment became

2

known. They encouraged the church by stating that they were certain the Nash portico could be preserved while the rest was rebuilt. Hopes were high. Surely there was a way forward here – if the church really wanted it?

2 The Man for the Job

> *There is an element of hypocrisy in demanding that the church must bring itself up to date and relate itself to the modern world, and then . . . insisting that it does its work in ancient, unsuitable and expensive buildings.*
>
> John Stott

'Pray as if there is no such thing as work and work as if there is no such thing as prayer' was an old saying which summed up the church's attitude to the now-public matter of the project. It was nurtured with much prayer, hard thinking and hard work.

It was soon clear that some full statement would need to be made to the whole church at the April 1971 Annual Parochial Church Meeting. To prepare for this there was a call to prayer and the first of several prayer meetings was held. Secondly, to aid everyone's thinking, a helpful summary was prepared in a paper entitled 'Which Way Forward?' It listed seven alternatives which appeared feasible:

1. To totally rebuild All Souls – 'a London property company has offered to completely rebuild on the site of All Souls at no charge to the church. This scheme would possibly include a new church seating 1000 people, church hall and lounge, restaurant facilities, meeting rooms for teaching and training, car park, staff accommodation with a hotel and office block above'.

2. A total rebuilding that left the rotunda intact.

3. Exchanging the site which was worth three-quarters to one million pounds. The building could be sold as a Nash Museum (perhaps) and an equivalent site purchased.

4. Rebuilding the daughter church of St Peter's, Vere Street – 'this could be a dual purpose building to include a chapel and a hall . . . depending how high one could build'.

5. Building over All Souls.

6. Adapting the interior of All Souls 'by removing the pews and using more flexible seating, or by lifting the floor to gallery level . . . the space underneath could be utilised as a hall and meeting rooms'.

7. Adapting the interior of St Peter's in a similar way.

Opposition to the idea of changing All Souls was beginning to come not only from outside by this time. Some members seemed to think, wrongly, that the idea was solely the creation of Michael Baughen. Because they were not too keen on new-fangled notions, they opposed him as well as it.

Others were against the idea for more understandable reasons. They had seen the battered and burned shell of the bombed church in 1940 rebuilt, restored and eventually re-opened in 1951, after ten years of worshipping at St Peter's. It seemed hard to see All Souls altered and knocked about again while they had to worship elsewhere. Some with architectural insights were aghast at losing the only Nash church in existence, and the last genuine example of his genius left in Regent Street.

John Stott tried to set the record straight by making a statement in which he explained that the original idea of radically changing All Souls had been his. He referred first to his much publicised remarks in Australia earlier that year, that a bomb on the church might helpfully sort out a few problems:

'Was I guilty of an unpardonable philistinism? I think not. I love All Souls. I have a sentimental attachment to it also. Not only have I been rector for twenty years and curate for five before that, but my sister and I were taken to All Souls on Sundays as children. We sat in the gallery, and misbehaved. I can distinctly remember making pellets of bus tickets and dropping them on the fashionable hats of the ladies below.'

He went on to summarise the church's dilemma: a large congregation, too little room, few modern facilities, no hall, and costly upkeep for a few hours' use each week. Then he concluded:

'Only a radical solution will do. We should be granted permission to demolish All Souls Church, preserve the rotunda and redevelop the site . . . Why should there be a public outcry? The public cannot have it both ways. There is an element of hypocrisy in demanding that the church must bring itself up to date and relate itself to the modern world, and then effectively stopping it from doing so by insisting that it does its work in ancient, unsuitable and expensive buildings.'

But despite this statement and John Stott's support, it was not an easy time – for Michael Baughen in particular. Much criticism came his way for wanting 'to change everything'. The unkindest and least creditable effort was a particularly nasty anonymous letter, which gave the impression that the writers had insufficient courage to speak openly.

And yet – as many people seemed to forget – John Stott had been the driving force, not only behind the rebuilding proposal but also behind Michael Baughen's appointment. It had been John Stott who had burned the midnight oil in Manchester persuading a rather reluctant Michael Baughen to accept the call to All Souls. If the appointment had been a mistake – whose fault was it?

Somehow the church weathered these stormy waters and with Michael Baughen still at the helm and John Stott supporting him to the full, they pressed on with two particular 'ways forward' from Michael's list of seven: the complete redevelopment of All Souls site; or, a poor second; using St Peter's church adapted for dual use as a church and a hall.

Once again the project ground to a halt. This time it was the Church of England, in the shape of the then Bishop of London, Robert Stopford, and the Archdeacon of London, Samuel Woodhouse, who told John Stott, Michael Baughen and the churchwardens that they thought it extremely unlikely that any such complete redevelopment of All Souls would come to fruition 'in our lifetime'. Any attempts to alter the outer structure of the church would be detrimental to its public image.

Yet that same meeting, which confirmed that the cheap way out of the problem would have taken too long to bring to pass in the light of the urgent pastoral needs of the church, was also the moment when positive encouragement came from both churchmen for altering the interior in some radical way.

Moreover, an architect's name was recommended as one who had the background and ability to do an expert job and yet meet the requirements of bodies such as the Council of the Georgian Society (guardian of Nash's architecture and Regent Street in particular) the Arts Council, and the Diocesan Advisory Committee (acting for the Chancellor of the Diocese). The architect was Robert Potter, F.R.I.B.A., F.S.A. of Brandt Potter and Partners, Southampton. More, Robert Potter's name commended itself to All Souls clergy and church council for a variety of reasons. His gifted designs for restorative architecture were amply evident in Bristol, Oxford, London and elsewhere. His work had been carried out in a number of distinguished settings – such as Chichester Cathedral, the conversion of All Saints Church, Oxford, into the Lincoln Library, and All Saints, Clifton. Furthermore he was an expert on stone preservation. A delightful asset to his work was that his wife, Margaret, a design consultant in her own right, often worked alongside him.

It was also of some significance that he was the architect of a very modern and unusual new church complex, the

Millmead Centre, the new home of Guildford Baptist Church, where a well known evangelical preacher, the Rev. David Pawson, was minister of an active and flourishing congregation. The Millmead Centre included not only a triangular church building with semi-circular tiered seating, but also halls, refectory, offices and a badminton court.

The arrival of Robert Potter on the scene was a major turning point in the All Souls rebuilding saga, and occurred just at the point when Michael Baughen was sharing with the church's core of lay leaders (known then as Commissioned Workers) his Bible readings on Moses. In these he expounded the principles of faith in a great God, what it meant to follow when the Lord led his people out, how this had to be matched with real prayer and how it called for unswerving faithfulness in his people. Naturally such principles could be applied to the challenge now before All Souls. The promised land – a dim vision to Moses and the Children of Israel when they left Egypt – represented the distant promised land of a new interior for All Souls. Many were to be the wanderings, the joys, the failures and the gathering of manna and fresh hope, as God provided the energy to press on against the odds. No one had any idea of the incredible story yet to unfold – it all seemed well nigh impossible. And Michael, as an added incentive, reminded the church leaders of Hudson Taylor's famous dictum that with God's work there were three stages: impossible, difficult, done.

This then was the challenge. To meet it, Michael pleaded, the whole church must get behind the proposed project in prayer. It was wrong to go ahead if it became clear that God had other plans, and useless to press on if the church leaders had to drag the rest of the congregation along willy nilly. He would not feel able to remain as vicar if the prayer meeting did not become the vital artery of the church's life.

In some measure, this longing for a more committed family gathering each fortnight was slowly becoming a reality. The meeting, previously rather formal with people in rows facing front, now had a welcoming feel as members faced each other in circular formation. Attendance was growing too, along with interest in the project. Soon numbers were so large, latecomers had to sit on the floor and ventilation became quite a problem in the old Waldegrave Hall's airless basement. The need for a bigger hall was becoming more acute and progress the more necessary.

One major way of discerning the will of God was to 'try the doors' to see what closed and what opened. The next 'door' to be tried was that of St Peter's, Vere Street. Was it the answer to the church's needs? An architect with a practice in the parish was commissioned to draw up plans for the adaptation of the St Peter's building.

Some of the problems that faced him would confront the future architect of All Souls. St Peter's was a historic building also: a beautiful little church designed by Gibbs and opened in 1724. Special architectural features included Burne-Jones windows, exquisite carving and moulding on the ceiling and chancel arch. Fixed pews and choir stalls hampered its use as a hall and would have to be removed.

These plans having been accepted at the July 1971 meeting of the church council, it was something of a shock to have them unanimously rejected by the Diocesan Advisory Committee in September. The possibility of using St Peter's as a hall took a knock – unless – as the D.A.C. suggested – Robert Potter was appointed as architect of both St Peter's and All Souls. Was that door closed or should it be pushed harder?

Whatever the answer to that question, thinking about All Souls itself was progressing. In late October at an evening service and afterwards, Robert Potter was introduced to the church family. It was quite a meeting! The architect had spent some time doing a photographic survey of All Souls and now explained some of his tentative plans based upon them. These seemed in some brilliant way to restore the simplicity of Nash's square building and for some members of the congregation it was a revelation.

Nash had concentrated, it seemed, on packing in the 1,500 people specified by the Church Commissioners: the

24

rich in rented pews, benches up the back of the gallery and against the walls downstairs for the poor. Sadly, by 1951, the only Nash furnishings left by the Victorians and the bombing were some of the short balusters to the low communion rail, the marble font and part of the organ case in the west gallery.

The decision to appoint Robert Potter as architect for All Souls was taken thereafter with enthusiasm and some excitement. But needless to say, the earlier plans for the alterations to St Peter's could not be dropped without further thought. There was some dissatisfaction with the Anglican powers-that-be at this stage. It seemed as if they were trying deliberately to thwart any hope of developing a hall within St Peter's, even though the need was so great.

Again the church put to the diocese their plan to convert St Peter's for a dual purpose. Once again the plans were rejected. It appeared that the interior of the church must not be changed because of its historical value – an example of Gibbs's work before he built St Martin's-in-the-Fields. Michael Baughen and John Stott could be forgiven for feeling somewhat frustrated in their attempts to make sensible use of money and buildings in the service of God!

They were not alone. The Bishop of Taunton writing in *The Times* in September under the heading 'Tombs – or Living Shrines' raised the same issue of having to keep buildings exactly as they were because of an exaggerated veneration for the past. 'This modern notion that everything in a church must remain unchanged sometimes rules out the possibility of encouraging intelligent worship inspired by contemporary insights.'

By January 1972 a further decision about St Peter's had to be taken. Still uncertain why the removal of the pews could not be allowed, the Bishop was to be consulted. Meanwhile it was agreed that Robert Potter should become architect also of St Peter's, Vere Street.

One of Potter's many admirers who rejoiced to hear of this double appointment, was the secretary of the D.A.C., Archdeacon Samuel Woodhouse. It had been he who had suggested his name in the first place at that earlier meeting. 'I am convinced he is one of the best architects in England,' he enthused. 'It was the best thing All Souls could have done. He is a keen churchman, a man of fertile imagination and ability. I knew he really could do it, and when he was appointed, I just said "Thank God!" It was the Lord's doing, I believe.'

But even Potter's appointment to both churches did not clear up the indecision about adapting St Peter's immediately. A work study group, set up to look at the future functions of the two churches, reported in March at some length and their preliminary thinking contained several significant pointers. The seventh 'ideal facility' needed at All Souls was a hall and restaurant. The hall needed to seat 300 with a projection room, stage, well-equipped modern kitchen and adequate toilet and cloakroom facilities. 'If a direct entrance from the street could be provided independent of those from the church (i.e. if the hall were underneath the church) it could be used for evangelistic out-reach.' Prophetic words, as it transpired.

Later in the same report, John Stott, its compiler, dropped a hint that was to add new urgency to the whole matter. The life of the old Waldegrave Hall in Duke Street, for so long the church's week night home, was limited. Moreover its image was too antique, its situation too distant and its availability too restricted for All Souls' continued use.

Surely now permission for St Peter's to become available for use as a hall would be given. If not – towards what alternative was God pointing the church?

3   Hidden Miracles: Phase One

> '*Dig out your own earth – it's the best and cheapest solution*'.
>
> Estate Agent

One misty April day in 1972, a small group of men could be seen gathered on the pavement on the south side of All Souls Church. Having removed the concrete paving one man, wielding a spade, began removing the soil from beside the church wall with some care, watched by Robert Potter, at whose instigation this 'dig' was taking place.

When the first foot or two of foundation brickwork was revealed, his face registered little surprise. As the next foot or two became visible he stepped nearer in some interest, expecting at any moment to see the edge of the foundation squared off. But the man was still digging – and as his trench grew deeper and more dangerous, Potter's expression was now a mixture of delight – at the unprecedented depth of Nash's foundation – and concern lest the walls of the trench were to collapse on the valiant digger. When at last the brickwork ended and only subsoil and rubble came to light, the hole was over thirteen feet deep and the lone workman almost out of reach when it came to handing him down a ladder to climb out.

Potter's pleasure at this unexpected find can easily be imagined, for there had as yet never been any reason to suppose that Nash's foundations were so deep. Those for St Peter's, for instance, were not more than three feet. However, it was more than likely that owing to the church being built on poorly drained land – where water and swampy soil could undermine it – foundations of an exceptional depth were laid.

Robert Potter's pleasure was of course shared by Michael Baughen and John Stott, and the church council when they met next on 4 May. If further digs confirmed (as they did) that the foundations were equally deep all round the church, there were, in effect, walls already present forming a potential 'basement'.

With the St Peter's redevelopment looking unlikely, and with the enquiries about other properties and sites being ruled out by astronomical prices, it was a major breakthrough to know that building underneath the church was at least a possibility. One estate agent expressed his view bluntly: 'Dig out your own earth – it's the best and cheapest solution.'

Meanwhile, the council had paid a visit to Guildford Baptist Church's newly opened Millmead Centre. It was not only Potter's design that fascinated, the members were glad to hear of God's leading of another group of his people into a faith project. When faced with raising a large sum of money, spiritual commonsense there had helped to balance weekly, sometimes daily, prayer meetings against the challenge to each member to be responsible for raising £50 towards the final total of £120,000.

These ideas were similar to the faith principles which Michael Baughen had already been expounding and which he had seen adopted to God's glory in a building project in his Manchester church. There the amount involved had only been £26,000, but it had been a 'mountain' for the church to face. They had trusted, prayed and put God to the test, and he had been absolutely faithful in bringing them through to completion in nine months free of debt.

Prayer was essential at All Souls too and on 4 June another Sunday afternoon meeting for special prayer spread the whole building project before God. There appeared to be three 'ways forward' by this time – altering St Peter's, raising the floor of All Souls to gallery level or excavating

28

beneath the church. All needed careful exploration and costing.

One of the most significant events in the project was the Church Council's annual day conference in September 1972, spent as usual in the beautiful surroundings of a country estate in Buckinghamshire. There were, as usual, a log fire in the hearth and coffee to be drunk on the terrace, lawns to stroll across and streams to walk beside. But the rest of the proceedings were to be anything but usual.

As the Council discussed and shared Robert Potter's thinking thus far, there came to everybody the deepening conviction that 'the Lord is in this'. No human engineering of 'atmosphere' had done it, nor any great sense of expectancy. Almost unexpectedly it became a key day when God set his seal on the venture in answer to prayer.

This is how Michael described it to the church family in the annual Gift Day letter in November:

'As we gathered for our Day Conference we had done our "homework" but had no clear solution or clear conviction about the way forward. Many people were praying for us ... We looked to the Lord for his hand upon us and he most graciously met with us. It was as if our plans and thinking were the laid fire – paper, wood, coal – and that there, in the conference, the Lord set it ablaze. Cold plans became living plans; schemes and ideas lit up for people; the feeling of wonder turned to exhilaration. It was not that some new plan emerged, but rather that all that we have considered over the past years came alive with unanimous agreement about the next steps. So we believe that the lights have turned from amber to green.'

This optimistic forecast gives the impression that immediately the plans for the new All Souls became bricks and mortar. But that was very far from the truth. It was to be another two years before this would even begin to take place.

Instead, 'Stage One' as it was called – to improve All

29

Souls' facilities while awaiting the fulfilment of the greater dream – began to take shape. The lower room of Church House was completely renovated in an imaginative relaxed way, with hidden lighting, tiered seating, wall to wall carpeting and a new servery. The south aisle of the church was altered also, with Potter's agreement, into an area without pews, where coffee could be served after services. To keep costs down the latter work was done by members of the church.

Meanwhile, at All Souls life had to carry on, renovations or no. It was hard to realise at times that God had a great purpose yet to fulfil. The church prayed for the new developments – and got on with its own business.

The man most conscious of the church's needs and God's help at this time may well have been Robert Potter. He saw prayer answered again and again as he worked away at the plans, and readily testifies to the many occasions when God's timing had been perfect. One such incident occurred when he was 'worrying at' them, seeking to sense the 'feel' of the building so that his suggestions would have a rightness about them. He worked long hours, scrapping some of the earlier ideas and gradually coming to the conviction that what was emerging on his drawing board was 'on target'.

Armed with these drawings he and his wife came up to London from Winchester to attend evening service at All Souls, to find the church's former archivist, Raymond Luker, himself an architect, had decided to come also. Living out of town he was rarely able to worship at the church. But on this occasion, he had brought with him something that Robert Potter did not know existed – a redrawing of Nash's original plans. The comparison of these with what Robert had produced was undertaken in the church after the service, and brought a tingle of excitement to all concerned. For in some remarkable way Potter's sketches had wonderfully rediscovered the purpose behind Nash's thinking. God again was assuring the church that they were 'on track'.

The details of Potter's later plans are significant, for many of them feature in the final result. By this time he had

30

decided against raising the church floor to gallery level, despite Michael Baughen's keen wish that this should happen. The latter felt strongly that the ground floor of the church, which would then become the hall, would be light and spacious, easy to reach from the street, and visible to those passing by. But Potter's architectural eye for problems was drawn to the pillars stretching from gallery to ceiling. If the floor was to be at gallery level, these would almost certainly dominate the church and make the congregation feel as if it were sitting in a birdcage! Furthermore, too much seating would be lost beneath the galleries to make it feasible.

As an alternative and to aid integration between those sitting in the galleries and those downstairs, he had decided to raise the church floor a mere eighteen inches while raising the chancel area three feet. The west gallery was to be extended and the others re-raked, while the pulpit was to be central, though moveable. Tentative plans were included for excavating under the church, in order to have a large clear area between the existing foundations, though additional pillars might have to be installed. Just to help everyone's thinking the quantity surveyors estimated all this might cost about £450,000 including the necessary repairs to the exterior.

The new plans were shown to the Annual Church Meeting in March 1973 attended by an unusually large number of members who responded warmly to them, particularly when their closeness to Nash's original intentions was revealed. It was thought-provoking to realise that All Souls had been originally designed with the preaching of the Word as the central feature, for it had been built before the advent of the Tractarian Movement of the 1840s.

The specifications, in fact, which were laid down by the Lord Commissioners of the Treasury in their Million Act of 1818 (when they voted one million pounds towards the building of churches in new districts) were fairly inhibiting to any great creative achievement. The administrators required that these Commissioners' Churches be built 'with a view to accommodating the greatest number of persons at the smallest expense within the compass of an ordinary voice, one half of the number to be free seats for the poor . . . ' As John Betjeman remarks wryly in his book on Church Architecture: 'In short what was wanted was a cheap auditorium and whether Grecian or Gothic the solution seems always to be the same. The architects provided a large rectangle with an altar at one end in a very shallow chancel, a high pulpit on one side of the altar, galleries round the north, west and south and the organ in the west gallery,' adding later, 'the only scope for invention which the architect had was in the design of the portico and steeple.' What an apt description of Nash's All Souls, Langham Place!

With the Tractarians' new emphasis on tradition, liturgy and the celebration of Holy Communion, the Victorians changed Nash's interior, attempting to impose on a simple galleried hall, the liturgical demands of the growing Oxford movement with its robed clergy and choir in a clearly defined sanctuary area with the focus being upon the altar, as they called it.

Robert Potter felt these changes could be regarded as a failure, for they reduced congregational participation to those seated on the ground floor. Not only did he hope to return the church to its earlier pre-Victorian simplicity, but also to improve, so far as was practicable, the integration of the worshippers upstairs with those downstairs. He hoped that with a raised semi-circular chancel area cleared of choir stalls, and radial seating in the church, the effect of an amphitheatre – with as many as possible able to see and hear – would be achieved.

In order that the final architectural plans (to be approved for action in the autumn) were as comprehensive and exact as possible, the church gave itself to careful thought and prayer about its needs at a special day conference in June 1973 at Oak Hill College, North London. It was a lovely summer's day: perfect blue sky and trees in full foliage fringing the beautiful lawn behind the college. The

32

conference divided into groups, all of which met in the open air in different parts of the grounds – the chairman of each equipped with plans and details. The purpose of the day was to provide a more leisured opportunity for the congregation to share in improving these with suggestions for consideration, points of disagreement and freedom to air any strong feelings. In the cool of the evening everyone gathered for a time of prayer and commitment in the college chapel before returning to central London.

During the following week the groups sent in their reports. There was general approval for the idea of not having pews as at present and for seating the choir in the west gallery with the organ. Some people suggested that Westall's picture over the Communion table (reputed to have been given to the church by George IV) should be removed; others felt that fund-raising should start as soon as possible. In the end, a sub-committee of seven council members was asked to study the reports in detail to help Robert Potter with his final plans.

The next six months were to be vital to the whole project. Not only had Potter's designs and projections to be understood and approved by All Souls, they had also to find acceptance with at least three other bodies: the Diocesan Advisory Committee (guardians of the Church of England's interests), the Council of the Georgian Society (guardians of regency architectural interests) and Westminster City Council's planning department (guardians of the public's interest).

Many church members feared that any or all of these 'hurdles' might prove to be insurmountable. For the D.A.C. had several times previously rejected plans for altering All Souls or St Peter's. If the church was the only surviving church in Britain designed by Nash, the Georgian Society might refuse any meddling with its historic fabric. (They had already received a letter from one member who wanted to make sure they knew the full 'horror' of what was about to be 'perpetrated' at All Souls.) Finally Westminster City Council had to be absolutely certain that the restructured

3   33

building was safe for use by the public. There were various regulations to be met which ensured that the alterations in no way endangered its stability or increased the risk of fire.

But the project was never going to start – let alone reach that second or third hurdle – unless the church family was convinced that this was God's way forward. The plans had to be part of a God-centred prayerful certainty and commitment.

The weekly prayer meetings during August continued to focus prayer on this crucial matter, especially as the church council's meeting at the beginning of September 1973 became decision day for Potter's plans. On that evening, after discussion and prayer a resolution was proposed and passed unanimously 'that we apply to the D.A.C. for a faculty to adapt our buildings in accordance with the design plans presented to the council by Mr Robert Potter'.

Step one had been well taken. The months of waiting, planning and quietly pushing and praying for a way forward seemed at last to be coming to a successful conclusion. Within a few weeks a number of unexpected events changed the complexion of the whole project – but not before the church had been convinced that God wanted them to launch out on this alone.

First came the news that the Trustees of the Waldegrave Hall intended to close and sell the property in Duke Street which was so valuable to the church's week night programme. But this was only a hint of what was to follow. In early November 1973 at the end of the first annual Gift Day for the project proper, a slightly bemused congregation listened to the bald statement in Michael Baughen's sermon that the Hall had been sold and the Trustees wished to pay entirely for All Souls' new basement hall with the proceeds!

It seemed almost an anti-climax. Just as the church was gathering itself for a great push forward, here was a totally new source of income stepping into the breach. But any thoughts of sitting back and relaxing were dispelled by the sum of money still needed to complete the project: about £150,000. With a national economic and energy crisis boiling up as Britain faced a bleak oil-starved inflationary winter even that seemed an incredible sum to raise.

As if to set the matter in its proper perspective, John Stott impressed upon the church that day the theological reasons for the alterations. All Souls was a church for others and needed to be more welcoming and less ecclesiastical. All Souls believed in congregational participation in worship, and needed flexible seating. Finally All Souls believed that the sacred and secular should not be rigidly compartmentalised and there should be freedom to experiment in different forms of expression of worship.

After that memorable Gift Day few people doubted that the project could possibly fail. Indeed further encouragements came thick and fast. At the end of November representatives of the D.A.C. met Michael Baughen and John Stott to confirm that the diocese had given their unanimous approval in principle to the whole scheme. Hurdle one had been passed safely. Furthermore, the Council of the Georgian Society to whom Robert Potter had written and sent his plans, had given its warm approval. Hurdle two was successfully jumped. Hurdle three would take a bit longer.

All Souls, it seemed, was to have its new church hall after all. Not built round the corner on some (non-existent) vacant site which would cost the earth to acquire, but in its own bowels. It was to be, in the words of Dr David Trapnell, one of the churchwardens, 'our own bargain basement'. For in the circumstances, it was far cheaper for the church to excavate its own site than to buy a new one.

It was also a far more exciting and unique piece of engineering and building. Robert Potter had first hand experience of such an exercise, for he had, not so long before, had to convert the basement of a redundant church, All Saints, Oxford, into a library for Lincoln College. So he was well aware of the problems, not least the sense of claustrophobia that a basement hall could have.

But he and his wife were determined to make the new hall as pleasant and relaxing as possible and planned to combine excellent lighting and ventilation with attractive decor.

As the three-day week and the power crisis welcomed in a gloomy 1974, three exploratory holes were being dug in the floor inside All Souls to look at the base of the large pillars within the church, and to assess the quality and strength of the brickwork. Robert Potter and Ove Arup (the consultant engineers who helped construct the Sydney Opera House), were amazed to find not just straight columns and rough brick, but beautiful inverted arches between each column. What was more, they were very well constructed and well preserved, even after 150 years in London subsoil. There was no reason why they should not be a valuable feature in the new hall. The 'bargain basement' was going to have some exceptionally high-class and historic brickwork to make its new facilities even more exciting.

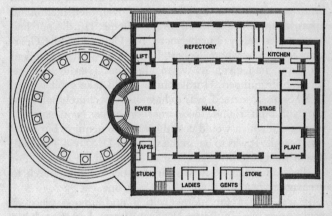

Plan of the basement hall and other facilities

4   Not All Roses

*All the congregation of the people of
Israel moved on from the wilderness
by stages, according to the command-
ment of the Lord.*

Exodus 17.1 (R.S.V.)

The discovery of those well-preserved arches seemed to set
the seal on the project architecturally. It was an auspicious
start to an otherwise depressing year, for the prospect of an
attractive underground hall was now almost a certainty. It
was the mechanics which had to be sorted out.

Arups subjected the foundations to extensive tests, but
could find no cause for alarm. The loadbearing qualities of
the 150-year-old brickwork were excellent. What possible
problem could deter the brilliantly-conceived plan from
completion now?

The answer was – many things. Uppermost in Potter's
mind was the rumbling already audible in the church every
time an underground train trundled past beneath, on its way
to or from Oxford Circus station. Imagine how loud that
noise would sound thirteen feet nearer and enclosed in a
space which could easily become one big resonance chamber!
If careful investigations did not take place there was also the
possibility that any new steel joists in the floor of the church
would pick up reverberations from passing trains and trans-
mit them up into the hall and church above.

An acoustics consultant was therefore asked to visit the
site. Professor Peter Grootenhuis of Imperial College took

measurements from the trial pits already dug, to discover where and how the sound was transmitted into the building. Ove Arup then made various suggestions based on his report, for noise prevention, ranging from surrounding the new hall in an acoustically sealed envelope (too expensive) to floating both the hall and church floor on rubber pads acting as shock absorbers, thus 'detuning' the steel girders with these 'baffling' insertions; the method eventually used.

That problem appeared to be overcome and forward-looking planning continued. All Souls would have to be closed for this major rebuilding task. Where could the congregation worship during the eighteen or so months it was thought the job would take?

Already the church leaders had been making enquiries, and three possibilities had been seriously considered: St Mark's, North Audley Street; St George's, Hanover Square; and the New Gallery Centre, Regent Street. The idea was to use St Peter's, Vere Street, in the morning when the congregations were usually smaller, and hire one of these other buildings for the evening service.

Three different groups from the church visited each of the suggested buildings, reported back that they favoured St George's. It was the nearest of the three to Oxford Circus and there were facilities for serving coffee after services. Yet, when it came to the moment of decision, the final vote was to use St Peter's for *all* services.

This change of heart, Michael Baughen explained, was not meant as a slur upon St George's who had been most hospitable and helpful from the start. 'But there was a desire that as a congregation we could feel free to do what we wanted in our own home, without fear of damage or disturbing anybody else's buildings or susceptibilities.' St Peter's would prove a very tight squeeze in the evenings, but it was the church's second home, acting as it had, in the war years, as a haven for the homeless All Souls family.

But adventures of faith are seldom smooth sailing as Moses discovered. Escaping from Egypt had been fantastic but there was going to be challenge after challenge ahead –

the Red Sea, the provision of water and food, direct opposition from the enemy, even attack from within the ranks of the people of God. Yet he learned to come back each time to ask 'Is this your way forward?' Impossibilities were turned into possibilities as God intervened. Problems were brought in prayer to the Lord and turned into a fresh deepening faith in God as God.

Time and time again the church family at All Souls would also be faced with crisis and find itself on its knees in thanksgiving for God's mercy and in petition for his answer to problems.

On the day that Robert Potter had first inspired the church council with his draft plans he was nearly killed in a car crash. He had been ill and was still undergoing medical attention. Driving home with his assistant to Southampton, he fell asleep at the wheel of his car which left the motorway at speed and plunged down an embankment. Providentially he woke in time to bring the vehicle to a halt before it plunged into a ditch, and escaped serious injury. The church family had good reason to thank God for this 'escape'.

Much later in the project, during the actual reconstruction of All Souls, the chief painter had connected an electric boiler by long cables in order to have boiling water available high up on the internal scaffolding near the ceiling. At 10 p.m. that evening, when he turned on the hot tap for a wash at home, he realised with horror that he had not only connected the boiler but had left it switched on – with only a limited amount of water in it.

He hastily rang Michael Baughen who ran all the way from the rectory to the church to pull out the cables and attempt to check the safety of the building in the dark. Next morning, the boiler was inspected and found to contain barely an inch of water. It seemed that God's overruling had prevented a serious fire from beginning. Once again the church family had cause for thanksgiving.

Meanwhile there was inflation which suddenly engulfed the nation and darkened the economic future. The alarming spiral involving colossal wage claims and rocketing prices was enough to deter anyone from thinking in terms of an expensive building investment. Yet surely God had been leading the church – could they stop now? Various ideas for raising money were discussed. Should the church use the services of a firm of fund-raising consultants? No. Should there be a national public appeal? No. Some ideas, however, were given positive support. Should there be pledges in units of £100 to help members assess what to give? Yes. Should there be a sub-committee to oversee the fund? Yes.

There were a number of accountants and brokers in the congregation whose advice and help was sought, but the task of fund treasurer eventually fell, perhaps surprisingly, to a research physicist, Andrew Scott. He had offered his services because of his experience in his work at University College, London, finding funds for million-pound international space research programmes. In the months to come, as estimates of costs rose, Andrew needed a cool head!

But the event which rocked the congregation most in 1974 was the news that the purchasers of the Waldegrave Hall had defaulted on the day before completion. Instead of £300,000 coming into the fund – there was nothing.

The most irritating factor was that, in order to give All Souls time to find a new week night home for its programme, the Waldegrave Hall trustees had given an extra six months' grace to their buyers. But that very six months had now put the church financially on the spot. For the national economic situation had suddenly deteriorated within just that period. With the three day week, the energy crisis and other economic problems snapping at its heels, the property market had collapsed and the resale of the hall was going to prove far more difficult.

The blow came also just as the project seemed likely to go ahead. Was this setback a signal that they were wrong to proceed? Maybe all the opposition stirred up within the church had a point? Was this the moment to call the whole thing off? Or was this a fresh challenge to faith in the living God?

40

The Waldegrave Hall became a recurring prayer topic over the months, for it represented the solution to what seemed an increasingly deteriorating situation. Yet as fast as possibilities for the Hall's sale occurred at strategic moments – they just as quickly evaporated again after the point of decision had been passed! Nothing else was to test the persistence of the church family's faith like this – again and again there seemed to be no answer. Even at the very last the sale of the Waldegrave Hall was to be the final symbol of God's faithfulness (but that could not be foreseen at this stage). As part of the bargain struck with the Trustees the new basement hall at All Souls was to be named the Waldegrave Hall, thus remembering the good works of an earlier generation.

For the closing of the old Waldegrave Hall at the end of April 1974 marked the end of an illustrious era for the former Gray's Yard Mission in Duke Street (founded in 1835 by Lord Radstock, the father of the Hon. Constance Waldegrave after whom the Hall was named) whose trustees were under a legal obligation to see that 'the Religious teaching given in the Hall or any part or parts of the said premises shall be confined to and strictly in accordance with the Protestant Evangelical Religion.'

Twenty years before, when the 110-year-old hall was derelict, dirty and disused – having served as an army drill hall during the Second World War – it had been discovered by a raw young curate newly arrived at All Souls, Langham Place, in 1945. One of the first tasks his rector had set him was the finding of a suitable hall for the congregation's use. For, in Harold Earnshaw-Smith's estimation, the whole work at the church was impeded and inhibited by this lack.

Early in 1946, John Stott began his search, visiting first the bombed site of St John's Church, Fitzroy Square, with thoughts of building a hall on the site. That was no good, so he started looking at existing buildings: auction rooms in Mortimer Street and a gymnasium in Great Portland Street. Still there seemed no answer to the need. It was on a foray further west, to a school in Barrett Street, just off Duke

41

Street, that the Gray's Yard Mission Hall was first mentioned to him by the school's principal.

Upon investigation the two big halls, one above the other, appeared to be not only vacant but also available. Moreover, negotiations with the trustees revealed that they were godly men concerned to see the Hall used once again for Christian work.

Knowing that St Paul's, Portman Square (as it then was), needed a hall also, John Stott talked to the vicar, the Rev. Prebendary Colin Kerr. Soon a management committee was in existence, made up of representatives of the two churches and the trustees, to oversee the renovations (paid for by the latter) and the subsequent letting of the hall to the two churches, three nights a week each. Because money to cover rent and upkeep was forthcoming from a daytime letting to the B.B.C., neither church had to pay for the facility.

It was in the Waldegrave Hall, then, that All Souls came to develop its programme of week night activities: The Wednesday Club, International Fellowship, and the Friday Fellowship. Then, in 1970, the trustees believed it was right, for reasons of good stewardship, to part with the increasingly dilapidated premises and put the money to better use.

The deeds stated clearly, 'the Trustees may at any time sell the said premises and shall hold the said purchase money in trust either to reinvest the same in or towards the purchase of a building and land . . . having regard to the purpose for which the building to be erected as aforesaid is intended to be used.'

All Souls Church certainly had a site and needed the money for a hall; the Waldegrave Hall trustees had the money (or so they hoped) and wanted to see another hall, dedicated to good works and the memory of the godly Hon. Constance Waldegrave. The two needs met and out of it grew a vision of a basement hall used not only by All Souls but also, it was hoped, by other Christian organisations who wished to hold large meetings in the West End – such as the Church Pastoral Aid Society, the Islington Conference, and others.

St Paul's, Portman Square, were informed of all these developments at an early stage, in case their need of a hall might prevent the plan from proceeding. But St Paul's had by this time a new church and hall of its own and no application was forthcoming from that quarter.

There seemed no let or hindrance in the plan which was put to the trustees in 1973. John Stott, however, who had been one of that number since 1949, was not prepared to influence his fellow trustees when this decision was put to the vote. It had been Michael Baughen, not he, who had first had the idea of offering the basement site at All Souls to them for their new hall. He was totally behind the proposal to offer the money in return, but he deliberately absented himself from the meetings when the crucial decision was being made.

He was therefore all the more disappointed that, six months later, when the last meeting in the Waldegrave Hall was held, there was so little to show for all the past negotiations and the forthcoming upheavals. An arrangement with the staff of the Whitefield Memorial Church in Tottenham Court Road, meant that the chuch had temporary accommodation for Tuesday and Thursday nights. But there was only a small proportion of the money that the trustees had hoped to give All Souls in hand, and little prospect of finding a buyer quickly with the now sagging property market.

So was the church still on the right path? Was God in this or not? Was there a cataclysmic disaster ahead – or was God's provision there in his timing – like the wells of Elim after the crossing of the Red Sea?

5   The Church Accepts the Challenge

> *Think of a sum of money, keep on in-*
> *creasing it until you reach the stage*
> *where it is too much, then stop – and*
> *you will find that you have the right*
> *figure.*
>
> Bishop Alfred Stanway

'Show me your ways,' prayed Moses when wondering if he
was still following the Lord's way in the wilderness. He left
behind the noise of the camp to ask that question. It was
time for the All Souls Church family to get away from the
bustle and pressure of London life to do the same. A church
conference week-end was planned for early May 1974 at
High Leigh, designed to be, as Michael described it in the
magazine, 'a time of coming closer together before we
plunge rapidly into the next two exciting and challenging
years as a church.'

But not even he realised that the week-end, planned long
before, would take place only a few days after the default-
ing of the Waldegrave Hall purchasers – an awe-inspiring
moment in the whole project. Could the church still go
ahead?

On 10 May two coaches and many cars left central
London for the drive out to the vast old house in Hertford-
shire. Despite one coach overheating and another not
appearing on time, eventually all the 150 guests arrived and
quickly settled in. The programme allowed for fellowship
and relaxation, but also for sessions when, as a family, the

44

major decision about the church's life could be aired at leisure and prayed through.

It was at the 'gloves off' session on Sunday afternoon that the full impact of what they had undertaken became clear. Michael Baughen explained the implications of the latest estimates of the total cost, the gloomy financial forecasts of inflation at two per cent a month and the rising costs. Finally, reminding the church that the faith-decision to go ahead had been made without knowledge of any money coming from the sale of the Waldegrave Hall, he warned of the possibility of not receiving any money from that source. What was the church's wish? Should the whole thing be called off altogether or postponed?

From all corners of the crowded panelled hall came murmurs of dissent. Then the questions followed, 'How soon can we start raising the money? What are we waiting for?'

Michael Baughen then outlined his provisional plan to launch the building fund in the autumn – with pledges leading up to the annual Gift Day in November. Reactions were spontaneous and unexpected.

'Why don't we start now?'
'What's the use of wasting three or four months?'
'Let's begin the building fund as soon as possible. We can't afford to wait.'

Numerous suggestions, but one thought: the church should begin immediately to put into operation the fund which was a symbol that the church family took seriously God's leading thus far.

Michael Baughen recalled his sense of amazement and joy at the congregation's enthusiasm. 'The church really pushed me into action when I wasn't ready to go. I was expecting the pledges to be made in the autumn and a slow build up to that. It was marvellous, though we didn't carry everyone with us.'

The High Leigh conference was considered a high peak in the project. The members who attended were ready to take up the challenge in earnest – or so it seemed. But it would be unfair to pretend that there were no doubtful or dissenting voices. Some had sincere and honest reservations.

There were those for example who had served abroad, maybe as missionaries, and had seen the needs of Christians in the developing countries. They knew how missionary societies in Britain, caught up in the inflationary spiral, wondered how they were going to pay their workers at home and overseas. Was all this expenditure on one church building right when the situation looked so grim?

Others had doubts because in comparison with many churches All Souls was well off. What about the millions of Christians who had no church at all, or had to walk miles to one? Was it a right use of time, money and energy in the light of the social needs too – not only of millions in the Third World but also in Britain, where poor housing, rising unemployment and the general lowering of moral standards seemed to have unleashed a tidal wave of permissiveness, violence, and homeless and drifting youngsters?

The sheer cost of the whole task – three-quarters of a million pounds – was enough to shake the resolve of others. Particularly when there was not even £20,000 in the fund to date! Any who were by nature cautious found it difficult to contemplate the demands of the next two years and what would happen if the money did not come in.

Still others found it hard to go ahead on this expensive project knowing that All Souls already had another building, St Peter's, which they thought might be used. Yet others were conscious of their neighbouring evangelical Anglican church down the road, St Paul's Baker Street. Could not a proportion of All Soul's flourishing congregation be of more use worshipping in the smaller church, thus relieving the pressure on the buildings in Langham Place?

More 'conservative' members who did not appreciate the changes in view, did not attend the conference at all. They wanted no truck with all this talk of a new building and money raising. Voting with their feet, they avoided as much as possible gatherings where the vexed matter was under debate. (Though some readily admitted later that they warmed to the project as it proceeded!)

For one fairly new member of the church council the turning point for his doubts was hearing John Stott reporting to the congregation on one of his overseas trips. 'He had been renewing friendships with people converted here at All Souls, or others who had been deepened in their faith while members of the International Fellowship. They were people of importance back home in their own countries – a bishop's wife in Iran, a group of church leaders in India and pastors in South East Asia. It struck me then that, in the light of All Souls' strategic outreach, spending the money on new facilities fell into place.'

For other people the crippling lack of a church hall was their particular turning point; the discovery that the basement walls necessary were already present helping to confirm that this was the right way forward now, despite inflation. Often, in fact, words of encouragement about the plans came from the least expected source: All Souls missionaries dependent to some extent on the church's generosity each year for financial help. Letters were beginning to come in as they read the January 1974 All Souls magazine, which gave full details of the project. Even some in Third World countries seemed to feel the money was going to be well spent.

High Leigh may have been a high peak in the project, but there was still some stiff climbing to be done. The nucleus of the church had agreed to press on and pledge. But that left a large proportion of the congregation wondering quite what was happening. In response to the insistence that something be started as soon as possible, the first appeal brochure, a yellow folded card entitled 'Share in the All Souls Building Project 1974-76' was designed and printed very quickly. It called itself a preliminary document outlining 'this strategic project and the prayerful and sacrificial commitment it demands'. The first Pledge Sunday, it indicated, was to be 30

June and further Pledge Sundays would be on 3 and 24 November.

Inside the brochure there was a brief outline of the way God had led thus far, then three sections giving details of the plans, the cost and the commitment needed to meet it. 'The sums involved seem enormous,' the section on finance read. 'Yet they have to be seen in relation to the enormous cost of building sites and rentals in the West End of London. To purchase a site large enough for a church hall would cost upwards of £2 million. Rental of buildings in the neighbourhood suitable for use as halls are around £50,000 a year, and rising all the time . . . This is not a restructuring for ourselves but for the worldwide work of the Kingdom of God, in which All Souls is so vitally involved.'

The preliminary brochure was distributed just nine days after the High Leigh conference at a memorable prayer gathering at which Bishop Alf Stanway (then Vice-Principal of Ridley College, Melbourne) spoke on 'Prayer and Projects'. It was unusual enough to have a visiting bishop speaking at the prayer meeting. In this case the relevance of his remarks to the fund's launch was the more amazing, for he had been booked to speak many months in advance when no-one realised how vitally important his words would be. These extracts may help to explain what I mean.

'I want particularly to speak about prayer and money, because you are going to be involved in asking God for a great deal of money. In one sense money is not very important; it gathers importance because the use of money is an indication of character. If we look at the sixteenth chapter of Luke's Gospel we shall find that the one who was unfaithful in that which was least was unfaithful in that which was most. If we cannot be trusted with that which is another's, because the money is not ours anyway (it belongs to God), who will entrust us with that which is our own? The right use of our money is an indication of character: faithfulness is a clear indication of our character also . . .

'When we are in a project, it is a great thing to ask God to encourage us. Sometimes people think that in order to be encouraged, we have to have a large sum of money. That is not true. Sometimes we can be encouraged by a very small gift, but I hope some of you are going to encourage your staff team by writing a note (you need not sign it) and say, "I have been thinking about this, and I am going to double what I am giving." Some might even treble it!

'I want to suggest that we should think out these things. First, we give ourselves to the Lord; the Christian life is ever a life of new beginnings. We give ourselves afresh to the Lord and say, "Lord, all I have is yours, so you make it plain what you want me to do, and I will do it." Think of a sum of money, keep on increasing it until you reach the stage when it is too much, then stop – and you will find that you have the right figure, a figure which you can give with peace and joy in your heart, and God will bless.

'Secondly, as we go on praying for the project we may find ourselves being called upon to give some more. Well, it is not an extraction, so let us do it joyfully. Do it and you will be able to pray for this project as you have never prayed for a project before. The amount does not really matter. The fact that it is a large sum of money has nothing to do with it; it is as hard to trust God for a pound as it is for a thousand . . . What really matters is that the project is in the will and purpose of God . . .'

With this challenge to each member to double his giving the first Pledge Sunday came round at the end of June. The result was disappointing. Not enough church members had had time to pray and think through the meaning of the pledges and only comparatively few were placed in the offering on that day. However, it was heartening to see that £66,000 had been pledged.

The Building Fund account was officially opened with £16,000 left over from the previous Gift Day plus £3,433.25 given to the Fund since. In every pew was placed the new golden-coloured gift envelope prepared by Michael Baughen. At the top of it was printed the verse 'That in everything He might be pre-eminent' Col. 1.18. Below it was the invitation – 'If you have any encouragement to share, or a comment – perhaps on how God has enabled or led you to give – please put a note inside with your gift.'

As if to make up for this initial lack of pledges, came the good news that Robert Potter's plans for the new building had been approved by the Planning Department of Westminster City Council. There were a few compulsory requirements, however, that would add considerably to the cost: provision of a lift to the basement hall and a toilet for disabled people. The third 'hurdle' had at last been safely negotiated.

Though Michael Baughen was understandably disappointed at the poor response to the first Pledge Sunday, his sense of God's purpose in this whole project – and his memories of his 'Moses experience' in Manchester – helped to steady his resolve; as it was to do on many other occasions during the project.

In fact, his first 'Moses experience' had revolutionised his whole ministry. In his first few weeks in his new Manchester parish he had had to prepare some Bible readings on Moses for the Oxford Inter-Collegiate Christian Union and was faced then with the challenge: was he serving the same God who led the Children of Israel into the promised land? For his new charge had certainly presented him with some problems.

At Holy Trinity, Platt, he had become rector of a small church with less than 100 in the congregation (later to grow to 500 or more). They were used to a staid 1662 Prayer Book tradition though their hearts were alive to the Lord. The church building was tall, narrow and seemed to cram in on him with its dark stained woodwork. Furthermore there was an 'absolutely ghastly' church hall!

It was to this overwhelming situation that Michael returned after giving those Bible readings. His mind was occupied by such questions as 'Do I believe God can do the same things today as he did then for Moses?' He commented later 'I believe God allowed me to hammer out these faith principles in the course of building the new church hall at Manchester not only to help the church. I had to prove that God was able . . . for my own sake in the ministry.'

The cost of the project in Manchester was £26,000, which might sound ludicrously small compared with £750,000, commented Michael. 'But to us then in Manchester it was just as big a mountain. I lost a lot of sleep . . . I used to wake up in the middle of the night in a cold sweat thinking about the building project. It was the first time I had led a church out in a faith project where big money was involved; where builders had to be paid – and, if the project failed, it was going to dishonour God.'

In his study of Moses he had seen God leading his people forward then back came the spies with their gloomy reports. 'They looked at the problems and not at God. The lesson was – to see God and then see the problems in perspective . . .

'In Manchester we reached the point of saying the amount to be raised doesn't matter – it is whether God is in the project, and whether the principles of prayer and faith are at the centre and the church, as the people of God, is going into the thing together in sacrifice and love for him.

'In many ways that experience in Manchester was a kind of apprenticeship for the building project here at All Souls.'

Michael Baughen's conviction was that the principles of the project at All Souls were no different from those he had followed at Holy Trinity. When faced with the gloomiest of forecasts in the summer of 1974, All Souls Church looked at the greatness of God and not at the magnitude of the problem. Believing God was leading them forward, the church began in earnest its two year pilgrimage of faith.

6 Into the Unknown

*You either screamed with frustration
or you laughed.*

Michael Baughen

'Dear Mr Baughen, I have just started teaching and as
rents, season tickets, debts from student days etc. are
taking all my wages at the moment, it is not possible for
me to fill in a pledge form as I probably would not be
able to keep it.

'However the vacation job I had at British Home
Stores is still open to me and I can and am working on
Saturdays. As I enjoy the work a great deal, that is my
reward and taking payment is being greedy – therefore I
intend to send what I earn to you for the building
fund ...'

'Dear Michael, At the end of term I received a cheque as
an honorarium and my intentions are to give the whole
to All Souls Church for the building project ... When I
came to London just over a year ago, I believed in God,
but it was not until hearing John Stott's sermon "The
Dread of Death" that I opened the door of my heart to
Jesus Christ. I just cannot put into words what happened
to me. I felt Jesus say, "I am ready to come in when you
open the door." '

'This gift comes with many happy memories of All Souls
Holy Communion during the blitz – and taking lunch
hour services at St Peter's (I was going to ring the bell for

52

one of these but by God's guidance was told it was the first day when church bells were to be rung *only* for an invasion!).'

These are but three of the many letters that were beginning to come in as news of the building fund's launching spread. Young and old – newcomers and oldcomers – were pleased to be part of what All Souls was doing. And not only individual responses encouraged the church. Among other organisations, three of the Oxford Street stores who were served by the All Souls chaplain were to give substantially towards the very essential redecoration of St Peter's in readiness for the move out of All Souls in 1975. In fact, the last six months of 1974 were filled with preparations of varying kinds – with a number of important events dominating many people's minds.

In order for the decorations and repairs to be done, St Peter's had to be closed from 1 August and its chancel area cleared of choir stalls, lectern and pulpit. It had been arranged that they should be stored in a church in north London and a lorry was hired to transport the items. But that was the easy part – actually physically getting them on and off the vehicle was another matter! Michael asked some of the staff to help.

Any stranger peering into St Peter's, Vere Street, on that occasion might have been forgiven for demanding to know what a group of labourers in casual clothes were doing collapsed on the floor in paroxysms of mirth around a horizontal pulpit. Michael Baughen would probably have explained that the said object was so heavy, and he and his fellow clergy had tried so hard to move it without effect, they'd got to a point of helpless laughter. 'You either screamed with frustration or you laughed – and we did the latter – especially when the others thought I was trapped underneath it!'

By the summer, too, preparations were well in hand for the major celebrations planned to mark All Souls's 150th anniversary in November. To help the building fund, and provide an outlet for many members who had little money but lots of talent, Mary Boon, a long-standing member of the church and council, was busy organising an exhibition of arts and crafts. Over the months she had gathered a team of stallholders who were in their turn collecting volunteers and materials for their different categories, from the youngest members upwards. In the normal course of events, All Souls did not go in for 'sales of work', so all this creative activity was fairly unusual and created a sense of involvement and excitement.

Special services for Sunday 24 November were also being planned – Holy Communion in the morning and a Sunday evening of praise and worship which was to include a musical drama presentation entitled '150 years'. Before this happy anniversary took place, however, the Church Council's annual day conference faced some heart-stopping decisions in mid-October.

There was no denying the magnitude of the resolutions to be passed at that conference in October 1974 held in Latimer, Bucks. 'It was a nerve-quivering day – because the realism of the figures for the project were laid before us,' Michael Baughen recalled. 'We were faced with a possible final bill of £750,000 and on that day the fund stood at about £26,000! Even if the church pulled back at the brink, having asked the architect to go to tender, this would involve a sum of money upwards of £50,000.' Moreover, the sale of the Waldegrave Hall seemed no nearer than six months earlier when the other purchasers had defaulted.

The council listened gravely to Robert Potter and the quantity surveyors explaining, sorrowfully, why the figures had leapt up so alarmingly from the previous £350,000. They were making allowances in this latest estimate for various inflationary increases, during the period of tender and building. But who was to say that their predictions were not over optimistic?

The visitors withdrew from the council meeting and the members settled down to pray and think through their present position. Was it right to commit the congregation to spending even £50–£60,000, let alone £750,000, with so little money in hand? Even though many 'giants' had already been overcome, in the obtaining of official blessing from the Georgian Society, the Diocesan Advisory Committee and the Westminster Council Planning Department, should all this money be spent on the church's own comfort? 'But it's not for our comfort,' others replied. 'It's for the gospel's sake.' 'Can we afford *not* to proceed?' one of the churchwardens asked.

The nub of the problem was still the lack of a hall. What alternative was there for the church if the decision went against the project now? The Waldegrave Hall was no longer available; and the Whitefield Hall was on loan for only a limited time. Where else could the church live like a family? Where would they welcome visitors needing Christ?

Finally, it became clear that the majority agreed. 'If we stop now, we could be failing the God of Moses and Joshua. We must believe He is able and "get our feet wet" as we go ahead by faith, not knowing how, in the present economic crisis we will raise the money.' When the vicar proposed: 'We affirm our belief that God has led us thus far and that he is well able to bring the total scheme to fulfilment to his Glory and in confident prayer and expectation of this, we resolve to authorise the architect to continue proceeding to the tender stage,' there were only two abstentions from an otherwise unanimous vote in favour.

Now that the matter was clinched – until Decision Day either confirmed or revoked it – all speed and energy had to go towards raising the money. For on 1 April 1975 the tenders would be received (and the preparatory work would have to be paid for). While on 15 April the final step could be taken only if at least half the money was in hand or promised. The long road stretched ahead with twists and turns that could not be foreseen. God's way of bringing the whole to completion was hidden from view. Nevertheless there was that exhilarating conviction that All Souls was about to witness some amazing answers to prayer.

Two major items had to be set in hand immediately: the

55

annual Gift Day letter and the official appeal brochure; both delayed in part until the financial situation had been clarified at the day conference. The church could hardly appeal for money without giving some firm idea of the target – and the likelihood of a sum coming from the sale of the Waldegrave Hall.

The Gift Day letter was swiftly prepared to outline the project in time for the first week-end in November. 'The next five months are crucial for the building project at All Souls. On 1 April it is expected that the tenders will be received. At that point we must have a sufficient proportion of the necessary money in our hands to enable the contractor to commence. Humanly it seems impossible. This drives us to our knees in prayer. We believe the Lord has led us into this project and our trust is in him as the one able to do "far more abundantly than all that we ask or think". He is the God of the impossible. The glory will be his.' Full details were given of the financial commitment needed, some background information and details of future hopes, before the challenge – to give – to covenant – to pledge – to sell antiques – to pray – was issued.

Behind the scenes in the early autumn the official appeal brochure had also been taking shape – in the minds at least of one of the curates, the Rev. Nick Wynne-Jones, and his design team (who handled the church's publicity) which included Dick Shepley and Mike Elkan (architects) and Peter Dunstan (interior designer). Meanwhile, under the eye of Michael Baughen and John Stott, the various items of information, explanation and letters of commendation for use in the brochure were being collected together.

From the former Bishop of London: 'I am very glad that a scheme has now been prepared which will both improve the building of the church itself, and also give adequate space for the congregation's groups and committees to meet ...'.

From the Archbishop of Sydney, Australia: 'I am glad to commend the Appeal now being launched on behalf of All Souls Church. I first had the privilege of worshipping there

56

in 1938 when the Rev. Harold Earnshaw-Smith was rector. Since then on various occasions I have shared in a service and preached at All Souls.'

The present Bishop of London, Gerald Ellison wrote: 'The parish has taken on a tremendous responsibility and it is the duty of all of us to help them in this courageous planning.'

The Bishop of Kigezi, Uganda, Festo Kivengere: 'I can only say thanks be to God who has allowed the knowledge of himself to spread like a fresh fragrance through All Souls unto the utmost parts of the world. I consider it a great privilege to be connected with this worthy cause "for his sake".'

Mr Chua Wee Hian of the International Fellowship of Evangelical Students: 'Our prayer is that God will continue to bless All Souls, and will use the proposed extended facilities to enrich not only the West End congregation but also strategic sectors of his worldwide Church.'

And last but certainly not least, Dr Billy Graham: 'It has been my privilege to both worship and preach at All Souls, Langham Place, and I have a great love and affection for the church, its people and its ministers . . . I am most honoured to be associated with its proposed restructuring.'

Other information in the brochure included a simple outline of the church's desperate need for decent facilities. Among the questions answered was:

'How can you justify this expenditure in the face of world need? – We could not possibly justify it if we were an introspective community spending the money on ourselves. But we try all the time to keep before us the call of Christ to serve the world. Thirty-five of our members have been ordained to the pastoral ministry during the last eighteen years, and about sixty missionaries and missionary couples have gone overseas since 1951. Thirty are still serving there, with more on short-term assignments. Probably more than half our congregation turns over every two or three years. So we see ourselves as a training

57

centre, and are constantly and gladly sending people out to other countries and other churches.'

As the 150th anniversary drew near the final items of copy were gathered together for setting and proofing, while the layout was finalised and photographs and architect's sketches obtained. The brochure was essential for the build-up to the church's first major financial deadline – D Day 1975 – when 'The final decision to proceed will depend on our having received or had promised at least half the estimated cost by that date' as it stated.

7   150 Years Young

I have a dream of an expectant church . . .

John Stott

Mary Boon turned over in bed restlessly. It was Saturday morning and dark – so it must still be very early. A glance at her clock confirmed that it was 5 a.m. . . . She lay back wondering what it was that had been on her mind.

Ah yes! The Arts and Crafts Exhibition in about a month's time. Something had been nagging at her consciousness – with the help of her stalwart team of forty dedicated helpers every detail appeared to be under control – and yet . . . The exhibition would be arranged around the walls of the hall and on its stage. The centre of the large hall was to be left empty . . . That was what she had been thinking and praying about: some sort of centre-piece to convey the purpose and prayerful intention of the whole day.

Into her mind came a vivid picture of the sort of centre-piece she wanted – a large model of the church, lit up inside, revolving and shedding light all around as it did so. The more she thought about it the more sure she became that God wanted this to be the focal point of the exhibition . . . but how? Such a model was not in existence as far as she knew – she would have to start making enquiries at church tomorrow. She prayed that she would be led to the right person to help her.

At the evening guest service she found herself sitting next to a Rhodesian member who helped in his spare time at the

All Souls Clubhouse. Stewart Spence was an engineer and in the course of their conversation, he asked if there was any way he could help the 150th Anniversary Exhibition. 'You don't know anyone who would make a model of All Souls do you, Stewart?' Mary asked tentatively. Stewart did and volunteered himself – one of his hobbies was making models . . . all he needed was a plan and some time to get the measurements and the materials together.

Mary Boon was overwhelmed. Here was God's answer to her prayer. Soon, with the help of one of the church-wardens, she had acquired an architectural plan drawn up by Robert Potter for All Souls – and Stewart began to construct a scale model of its exterior. Fortunately he was able to get on with it in his spare time at work – receiving lots of advice from his colleagues – plus the invaluable offer of help with making the small windows which were essential if Mary Boon's vision of a building lighted from within was to become a reality. But it was very hard work to complete the task in time and fulfil his other commitments. He managed it, on the night before the exhibition, even down to the little torch bulbs wired up ready for use. When lit up the model looked just like All Souls did from outside on dark Sunday evenings.

An enormous amount of work went into the exhibition and sale and it was a marvellous time of sharing and fellow-ship – resulting in the raising of £2,700. Mary Boon's heart was very full at the end of the day – and for her especially the centre-piece had been particularly successful. 'For all of us,' she said, 'it symbolised our dream of light and truth and hope streaming out from our church in every direction to the ends of the earth.'

That week-end's worship and praise centred on the theme of thanksgiving – and dedication, not only to the building project, but also to God's call to serve His Son.

John Stott's contribution was to become much-loved and much-quoted. It was a look into the future entitled 'I have a dream . . . ' (with apologies to Martin Luther King and his famous Washington speech):

'I have a dream of a church in Central London which is
a biblical church –
which is loyal in every particular to the revelation of
God in Scripture
whose pastors expound Scripture with integrity and
relevance, and so seek to present every member
mature in Christ
whose people love the Word of God, and adorn it with
an obedient and Christ-like life
which is preserved from all unbiblical emphases, whose
whole life manifests the health and beauty of
biblical balance
I have a dream of a biblical church.

I have a dream of a church in Central London which is
a worshipping church –
whose people come together to meet God and worship
him
who know God is always in their midst and who bow
down before him in great humility
who regularly frequent the table of the Lord Jesus, to
celebrate his mighty act of redemption on the cross
who enrich the worship with their musical skills
who believe in prayer and lay hold of God in prayer
whose worship is expressed not in Sunday services and
prayer gatherings only but also in their homes, their
weekday work and the common things of life
I have a dream of a worshipping church.

I have a dream of a church in Central London which is
a caring church –
whose congregation is drawn from many races,
nations, ages and social backgrounds, and exhibits
the unity and diversity of the family of God
whose fellowship is warm and welcoming, and never
marred by anger, selfishness, jealousy or pride
whose members love one another with a pure heart
fervently, forbearing one another, forgiving one
another, and bearing one another's burdens

which offers friendship to the lonely, support to the
    weak, and acceptance to those who are despised and
    rejected by society
whose love spills over to the world outside, attractive,
    infectious, irresistible, the love of God himself
I have a dream of a caring church.

I have a dream of a church in Central London which is
    a serving church –
which has seen Christ as the Servant and has heard his
    call to be a servant too
which is delivered from self-interest, turned inside out,
    and giving itself selflessly to the service of others
whose members obey Christ's command to live in the
    world, to permeate secular society, to be the salt of
    the earth and the light of the world
whose people share the good news of Jesus simply,
    naturally and enthusiastically with their friends
which diligently serves its own parish, residents and
    workers, families and single people, nationals and
    immigrants, old folk and little children
which is alert to the changing needs of society, sensitive
    and flexible enough to keep adapting its programme
    to serve more usefully
which has a global vision and is constantly challenging
    its young people to give their lives in service, and
    constantly sending its people out to serve
I have a dream of a serving church.

I have a dream of a church in Central London which is
    an expectant church –
whose members can never settle down in material
    affluence or comfort, because they remember that
    they are strangers and pilgrims on earth
which is all the more faithful and active because it is
    waiting and looking for its Lord to return
which keeps the flame of the Christian hope burning
    brightly in a dark, despairing world
which on the day of Christ will not shrink from him

in shame but rise up joyfully to greet him
I have a dream of an expectant church.

Such is my dream of a church in Central London
May all of us share this dream
And under God may the dream come true!'

At the end of November when the sums had been done,
the building fund stood at almost £75,000 – the first tenth,
as Michael Baughen promptly dubbed it. The giving in that
month, £41,000, exceeded all previous efforts (averaging
£5,000 a month) with £21,000 alone on the Gift Day at its
start. Yet this was but the beginning.

Many novel ideas for raising money were beginning to
take shape involving members of all ages. Housewives and
mums took on Saturday jobs in order to have extra money;
older retired members went back to work again to earn
money to give. Many single professional members donated
all or part of their pay increase. Students took on vacation
jobs. Others found part-time employment. Many people
admitted that Bishop Stanway's words 'think of a figure and
double it' prompted them to dig deeper in order to see God's
glory. 'It was exciting,' one admitted, 'to write larger
cheques than one had written before . . . '

The children were not without ideas either. They contributed model racing cars, plaster models, wooden dice, lamp-
stands, candles and jewellery to the exhibition and other
sales, and were encouraged to bring homemade cakes and
sweets for sale at the prayer meeting – in aid of the fund.
The teenagers in particular gave an enormous amount of
time – and energy! – to doing a sponsored cycling marathon,
round and round Hyde Park, averaging between fifteen of
them some 30–40 miles each and raising about £350. One
who was not able to cycle gallantly walked the distance!
Another group walked the Pennine Way.

Sponsored slims and swims were also popular, for the
older and more active, and often a little thought and
lots of elbow grease earned an extra pound or two . . . like

the girls whose landlord wanted someone to clean the communal stairs to their block of flats each week. Some people with freelance earnings – royalties, fees, trust income or investments – made these over to the Building Fund. For many holidays, new clothes, expensive treats were out, and the money saved for the project.

As members gave each week, brief messages, often anonymous, gave some idea of the sense of joy they found in being part of the project.

'This is just a note to thank you all on the staff for making the six months I'll have been here so enjoyable. I know it's a small offering, but I hope it will be of help.'

'The enclosed 50p comes from an old lady to whom my parents gave an Appeal Brochure . . . '

'Our Fellowship Group spent a Saturday tidying the garden of a vicarage in the country in return for this donation.'

'A token of thankfulness to God, this is the fortieth anniversary of my becoming a Christian.'

'The Lord has given us great joy in choosing my fiancé and I for each other, with the additional blessing of allowing us to marry in All Souls. We give the enclosed as a token of our gratitude and love for Him.'

'This is the half-yearly interest on my deposit account and I wanted you to have it all for the Building Fund.'

'I re-calculated my tithing and giving over the last seven years and came to the conclusion that I'd been robbing the Lord of his due. I've signed a covenant form . . . '

'Some back pay I didn't know I was going to get and which the Lord has led me to give to the Building Project.'

'For the All Souls Building Fund, with grateful thanks to God for a tax rebate.'

'With grateful thanks to the Lord for all he has given me and for the wonderful way in which he has blessed me over these last few weeks.'

'Thank you Father for the joy of being able to do this . . . '

It was, as Andrew Scott soon realised, the faithful church members giving little and often by cheque from their current salaries, that made up the bulk of the giving.

After the Exhibition, and in order that those who had little in the way of money could still give of their time or talents, an ongoing scheme was created entitled 'Task, Talent, Treasure'.

'*Task*: if you have a professional skill which you are pre-pared to offer for spare-time work, you are invited to join our Task Force. Members of the church family and their friends will then be encouraged to call upon your services at the going rate, knowing that the job will be well done, but also that earnings over and above the cost of materials will be contributed to the Building Fund.

'*Talent*: With our many visitors particularly in mind, we are proposing to set up a small permanent exhibition/sale of arts and crafts, the entire proceeds of which will be contributed to the Building Fund.

'*Treasure*: In consultation with an expert adviser on antiques and valuables, we are prepared to receive gifts of this kind and obtain the best price for them – to be contributed to the Building Fund.'

In the third category, people generously gave treasures, furniture, silver, coins, *objets d'art*. Some were offered to antique dealers and auctioned or sold. One member who had bought an antique table for £4 was thrilled to see it fetch over £100 for the Building Fund when it was re-sold.

Altogether, the 'T.T.T.' scheme helped to raise a further £2,000, while two further sales of arts and crafts on a

5

smaller scale raised over £1,300. A recital given by music students in the congregation contributed £200.

The project was certainly teaching the church that, as Paul expressed it in 2 Corinthians 8, one of the marks of giving from the heart was 'abundance of joy'. So along with the excitement and joyful sacrifice there was always praise for the manner in which God had opened up ways to give, and thankfulness for the proof that God was no man's debtor. Everyone agreed it was a privilege to be part of it all. It was an on-going, day-to-day adventure seeing God at work. It was the non-givers who were missing out!

8   Decisions! Decisions!

> *The Lord seems to be leading us across a river by stepping stones. When we look back the stepping stones behind us have disappeared ... we must press on in faith and hope ahead.*

> Church member

On 16 December 1974 Michael Baughen found himself in an uncomfortable position. He had been reading in Mark's Gospel chapter eleven the story of the withered fig tree and Jesus's words, 'Have faith in God. Truly I say to you, whoever says to this mountain "Be taken up and cast into the sea" and does not doubt in his heart, but believes that what he says will come to pass, it will be done for him' (verse 23).

For Michael, as he meditated on these words and related them to the building project, the crunch seemed to be – how many decisions were being put off because Decision Day had been set as 15 April 1975? Faith entailed stepping out, believing now that the decision would be 'yes' *then* – in four months' time.

One step he personally felt had to be taken before it was too late was ordering the landline TV link from St Peter's to Church House's lower lounge. It was very unlikely that the whole congregation, as at present, could squeeze into St Peter's but with a TV overflow facility, extra people could be accommodated in particular for special occasions.

67

'I found myself convicted through the scripture that faith, such as the faith to remove mountains, is a faith without doubt. I became gradually aware that if we waited until the middle of April 1975 before we knew whether we were going to close All Souls and move to St Peter's at the beginning of May, it was obviously going to cause problems in all our planning. I thus came to the conclusion that we must proceed on the assumption that on 1 May 1975 we move to St Peter's, Vere Street. I propose therefore to the Church Council and all the team that we proceed on this basis . . . I have also taken action with the Post Office and asked them to proceed with putting in the landline link. They needed six to nine months' notice and I asked them if it was possible to do it by May!'

Thus wrote Michael Baughen to the staff team and the P.C.C. in January 1975, having consulted one of his church-wardens about the problem. His decision was not popular with everyone, however. One or two council members felt fairly strongly that they should have been consulted first. To Michael, however, it was an outward and visible expression of faith in God. It was significant that after the meeting when it was discussed the member who had opposed the vicar's decision most strongly went across to make it clear (with tears and a hug) there was nothing personal in their action. The love within the church family was here mirrored by the tiny nucleus of the council.

This incident was not the only remarkable thing about the deliberations. According to one younger member, when a vote in the church council wasn't unanimous, 'Michael Baughen came back (at least twice) to the next meeting and said he wasn't happy to go ahead after the previous meeting's divided vote and explained that new circumstances had totally changed the situation . . . He asked us if we were willing to vote again. At this second vote, the result was unanimously in favour.'

He recalled vividly also the comment of one member when the sale of the hall had fallen through: 'The Lord seems to be leading us across a river by stepping stones. When we look back the stepping stones behind us have disappeared. We tend to worry about this – yet what does it matter. They have got us to the place in the middle of the river . . . we must press on in faith and look ahead.'

By the beginning of 1975 the crucially important Covenant scheme for the Building Fund was also under way. Pioneered in particular by John Stott and his secretary Frances Whitehead, it resulted in some 400 covenants and would bring in (over seven years) between £60,000 and £70,000. Frances Whitehead was also responsible for checking through endless mailing lists of addresses of Friends of All Souls, former congregational register members, welcome cards filled in by visitors to All Souls, Ex-Fellowship Group members, magazine subscribers not on the congregational register, previous members of staff, those listed on the baptism, marriage and confirmation registers, and committee members, old and new, for the church activities such as the Philadelphian Fellowship, Wednesday Club, and All Souls International Fellowship.

Eventually the brochure was sent out on four main mailing lists and many hundreds of letters were written by Michael Baughen, Di Wheeler, Michael Baughen's secretary, John Stott and Frances Whitehead.

The congregation took up the load as well, sending or passing on brochures to interested friends and relatives. Michael Baughen and John Stott each had their own personal mailing also.

In the final planning the appeal was limited in two respects. First it did not include the very costly repairs needed for the exterior of All Souls, concentrating on the £650,000 for the interior only. Furthermore, the appeal would only be made to members and Christian friends of the church. It seemed wrong to ask for money from non-Christian sources for a building whose major task was Christian worship, evangelism and teaching. 'We wanted money given with love,' was Michael Baughen's reasoning.

Countdown to Decision Day on 15 April began in earnest

in the new year with a special Sunday afternoon of prayer in a very chilly St Peter's, Vere Street – not yet redecorated or ready for its new visitors; with gaping holes where new double glazing for the B.B.C. studio would be installed. Daily prayer meetings began also on 10 March. To help the final decisions about the tenders for the rebuilding on the day itself, the church was asked to give fresh pledges on the Sunday before, 13 April.

Meanwhile, to save deflecting money to be given to the thirty or more All Souls's missionaries during this vital period, the church's usual missionary gift day in March was postponed until June (but only with the stipulation that if there was less than the usual giving on that day, then the November Gift Day must make the balance).

It was thrilling to see the Fund exceed £100,000 by the end of February. The giving so far had been steadily coming in at the rate of about £4,000 a month – in the special gift envelopes placed in the offering plate, delivered by hand or sent through the post. Since November the monthly income had risen steadily: £7,000 in December, £15,356 in February, £20,000 in March. Pledges made in June 1974 were being fulfilled – while new ones came in from 1 March onwards.

The giving on the Sunday before Decision Day was £15,500, matching the total giving for the whole of February. But the Council prepared itself for all eventualities. They were made aware that if the ten tenders were too high, or insufficient money had come into the fund, the builders could curtail their activities accordingly. The site could be excavated, a new floor put in at the higher level, and the church move back in, leaving the underground hall to be completed later – which would reduce the cost to £200,000. But there were positive encouragements to go ahead as planned.

Following the line of Michael Baughen's faith principle, and boosted by the news that the Trustees of the Waldegrave Hall hoped to donate £100,000 to the fund by midsummer, John Stott made the following proposal: 'In the light of God's leading so far, especially in the remarkably generous giving of the congregation and the commitment of the Waldegrave Hall Trustees, the P.C.C. are clear that the congregation *must move* to St Peter's on 1 May. Although the final decision of how much work on All Souls can be authorised must still be made on 15 April, the Council authorise Michael Baughen, at his discretion, to go ahead with all essential expenditure which cannot reasonably be delayed until 15 April.'

Opposition to the new project continued right up to Decision Day. One member of the Council circulated the others with a lengthy letter in which he outlined his reasons for believing that God was not leading the church in this direction. If they agreed with him he hoped they would vote against the decision.

For most members the letter proved a helpful stimulus to thoughtful prayer – for it gave an excellent summary of the objections to changing the building. Having considered these carefully, the Council could make its decision with some confidence.

So there was no easy passage for the project even at this stage. But even Michael Baughen agreed that opposition helped to sharpen his own and the Council's thinking, 'though it made the going extremely tough!'

The Sunday before Decision Day, Michael Baughen asked the Council to meet informally – to look at the state of play, to consider lines of action and to pray about the decision to be taken that week. He repeated to them the words of Robert Potter, as he gave Michael some very encouraging news, 'The Lord is with us.'

On the evening of Decision Day itself Potter and his assistant were present to help the Council in its vital deliberations. It is noteworthy also that two of the members who were unable to be present wrote expressing their support. One was churchwarden Dr David Trapnell, involved in the redevelopment plans from their first inception, who was lecturing in Persia. The other was the one who had previously opposed the whole project and he wrote to say that

71

he thought the church should go forward now – but that he still had reservations about some aspects of the project.

Michael Baughen began with his explanation of the factors involved in the making of the decision, then turned to the good news about the tenders. Ten firms had sent in estimates for the major renovations, and even the highest was lower than expected! Factors beyond the church's control, such as the economic squeeze, inflation and the slump in the building trade, had made the firms eager for the job.

What seemed to make the tenders even more remarkable was that the lowest of all was from a highly reputable firm, J. W. Falkner & Sons Ltd of Ossory Road, London, who were experts in restorative and creative work of a high quality of craftsmanship, as evidenced in their current task, converting Holy Trinity Church, Southwark, into an orchestral rehearsal centre. Robert Potter and the quantity surveyors had no reservations in recommending them for the job.

This was great news! But what of the church's side of the bargain? The total to date for the building was estimated to be £162,173 in hand, plus promised covenant income of £25,000, the Waldegrave Hall's £100,000 and £60,000 newly pledged by church members. Add to that a further £28,000 promised and several other items and the sum would be £386,814, something like half-way towards the target.

But over and above Falkner's estimate, two major items of expenditure had to be remembered. The 1951 Willis organ needed a complete renovation that would cost a further £50,000, while the essential major restoration work being done on St Peter's needed in the region of £30,000, to allow the All Souls family to move there while the major rebuilding was done.

The Trustees of the Waldegrave Hall were once again the great source of hope, for a new offer had been made of £150,000 (considerably lower than the hoped for £300,000, but time was pressing). Perhaps it was right that negotiations should clinch this sale so that the money could boost the building fund to £536,814?

The historic proposal, made by Professor Norman Anderson, seconded by Dr Richard Bird and agreed immediately and unanimously, stated: 'We accept at once the lowest tender from J. W. Falkner & Sons Ltd . . . ' And afterwards the members of the Council paused gladly to praise God in a time of prayer and thanksgiving, before going on to some less straightforward decisions.

The uncertainty about the new sale of the Waldegrave Hall held them back from a total commitment to the organ renovations. Until the contracts for the sale had been exchanged no definite decision about the future of the instrument would be made.

The moment of truth had come. All Souls Church, Langham Place, was to be closed on 1 May 1975 and would never be the same again.

9 All Souls Celebrates

*Leave the possible things to un-
believers; tackle the impossible things
as believers.*

Brother Andrew

'As you will know from the title of this record, we are, in
fact, celebrating closing down our church building. It
seems a very strange thing to celebrate. Yet, although the
building may be closing temporarily, the church itself, the
real church, the body of God's people, is not . . . Because
God has led us to this point and has made the impossible
become the possible by his hand, that is why we are celebrating this evening . . .

'As a church family here at All Souls, down through the
many years, God has met his people with blessing, grace,
challenge and conviction. At this point in our history as
a church he has brought us face to face with the need to
develop our buildings in order that we can be more
effective here in the centre of London. As we come to this
evening, we are overwhelmed with the wonder of what
God has done.

'When we set our hand to this task, believing God was
leading us into it, inflation was so spiralling that most
people thought we were crazy. We were encouraged by
the words (I believe they are Brother Andrew's): "Leave
the possible things to unbelievers; tackle the impossible
things as believers." The impossible situation we faced was
the raising of an enormous sum of money – not knowing

74

how it would come, but believing God was leading us. Tonight we rejoice that though no human calculation could have shown how we could have come to this point quite so rapidly, God has solved it for us and shown us the way.

'Tonight, therefore, we celebrate the Lord's gracious overruling. It is to the Lord's glory that we ascribe our praise. He has honoured his word. We have stood upon his promises in Malachi 3, in Mark 11 and of faith. God has poured out his blessings and has removed mountains. He has proved his utter faithfulness. So that as we trust him and follow his leading, so he opens the way through the impossible.

'Thus from our hearts, the praise on this record is praise to Jesus Christ, the eternal Son of God, our Saviour and Lord.'

Thus Michael Baughen explained why All Souls was celebrating on the L.P. record made at the final service in the church before its doors closed on 1 May to allow the builders to move in. The disc 'All Souls Celebrates' made at the request of Word Records, went on to become a best seller, especially on the church bookstall and in the nearby Scripture Union bookshop in Wigmore Street. Royalties from it continued to flow in to the building fund in the following years.

Celebration was certainly its keynote with Noel Tredinnick, the church's Director of Music, and the full support of choir, orchestra and congregation, the excitement and zest of a church about to make a mighty leap of faith vibrated in every note – whether sung or played.

This major change of homes was not all singing, however. It was also backbreaking, dirty, hard work. First, St Peter's, only recently vacated by the builders and decorators, had to be thoroughly cleaned and prepared by church members for its new role. It was not the first time that voluntary helpers had been involved. All the rewiring of the smaller church had been done by volunteers, with Stewart Spence, the man behind the model of All Souls, once again using all his strength and engineering ingenuity to try to get the huge but antique ventilation fan hidden in the rafters of St Peter's to work. A new fan was the only answer, and Stewart spent several fairly dangerous hours crawling around the roof timbers installing it.

For most of the congregation, the great migration took place during the three days after the last Sunday in All Souls. Any member of the church family who could, took a day off from work because the double aim was economy and speed, in order to have St Peter's usable by Tuesday morning for the BBC's broadcast of the Daily Service. But that meant not starting until Monday's broadcast from All Souls was completed.

After that the heavy work began in earnest as All Souls was stripped ready for the workmen. The pews downstairs in All Souls were in solid fixed sections and proved difficult enough to manhandle. But upstairs in the galleries, where space was far more limited and narrow staircases had to be negotiated, it was far worse.

Having staggered down with the pews to the street level, the task was not over. They had to be loaded, with the pulpit, font, lectern and choir stalls on to lorries and unloaded again when they reached their destination in Fulham (an empty church used as a storehouse).

Back at All Souls and St Peter's, a tremendous job of clearing, stacking, sweeping, lifting and carrying went on. Members with cars helped to transfer the pew Bibles, hymn-books and service sheets in readiness for the next Sunday. At last, as darkness fell and the shops and offices around emptied, the verger, Arthur Carr, took a last look around his unusually spacious responsibility. Very strange it was, he thought, to see bare floorboards, metal gratings and raised wooden sections where hours before had been heavy wooden pews. He knew, though, that that dim interior would not be silent for long. Soon the hoardings would surround the church and porch and the men with the excavating machinery would move in, while the organ builders would begin to strip and take away most of the organ for storage. He glanced up at Westall's picture – he hoped they'd remember to board that up or there would be trouble!

Settling in to worshipping at St Peter's was probably not as traumatic as all the predictions had suggested it might be. Michael Baughen made the move a time for reminding members again that this might be the right moment for some to move away altogether. It was an accepted fact in the church that people ought to regard their time there as a period of training and spiritual building-up for future service in a smaller local church. 'Is God saying to you, now, "Move on"?' Michael asked. 'Is there a local church nearer home you should be attending and where you could become involved in worship and supporting its work?'

After a few Sundays at St Peter's, it was clear that many people had taken the hint quite happily, and gone elsewhere. Extra seating down the aisles, in the chancel area or up the wide staircases was not always necessary, and the drop in the weekly offerings confirmed that fewer people were present. Yet, St Peter's always seemed tightly packed – and no more so than in the tiny clergy vestry and the small sanctuary. On big occasions when the chancel was filled by choir and orchestra plus screen and projector for a slide sequence it resembled something more like an obstacle race than the front of a church!

Michael Baughen, for one, considered everyone had coped remarkably well. 'There were times at the front when one got almost to screaming pitch. Somehow we endured the enormous amount of inconvenience and I believe our time at St Peter's proved a success. We felt welded together as a family (and in the heat of two of the hottest summers on record was it surprising?). I know some found it too much for them, but the majority did not. We prayed that our time there would be of spiritual blessing and it was.'

Indeed, for the married couple who faithfully looked after the TV relay back at All Souls Church House each Sunday evening, the time at St Peter's was to prove of tremendous value also. John and Margaret Tear found great joy in ministering to the needs of the tiny group of regulars who attended. The latter always found a quiet comfortable hall in which to worship, carefully prepared beforehand by the Tears. The intimate surroundings reaped their own reward as strong bands of fellowship developed over the months. Newcomers and strangers were given an especially warm welcome. Often visitors who arrived too late to be re-directed to St Peter's naturally felt disappointed, as one Australian worshipper admitted later in a letter:

'I felt quite dismayed. Here I had come all the way from Australia and I was to watch the service on close-circuit TV. However, my let-down feeling didn't last long. There was a dear lady there who was so kind and loving to me. I noticed an atmosphere of warmth and friendship in that room as it filled. This lady came over to me quite a few times to see if I was comfortable. I wonder if she knows what that caring meant to me a stranger from a far-off country?'

For many younger members of the congregation, it was also the first time they had fully appreciated St Peter's as a building. Few regulars at Sunday services at All Souls ever entered St Peter's, because for the previous fifteen years its use had been limited to lunch time and communion services. Thus, to see the tastefully decorated ceiling (attributed to Bagutti), the Burne-Jones windows and the lovely plaster moulding, now well lit, was a surprise advantage from the closure of All Souls.

The move over, there were tough decisions still to be made about many items needed in the new All Souls. Undoubtedly the largest and most essential was the organ. It was clear from all the reports and enquiries made about possible solutions to the problem, that the church already owned a superb instrument – even though it was patently in need of complete overhaul. Furthermore, any modern electronic alternatives to the 1951 Willis were ludicrously inadequate in a church the size of All Souls.

78

By September the issue could not be shelved any longer. Harrison and Harrison, the Durham firm of organ builders, would not be able to do the job in time if the go-ahead was not given soon, for their future schedule was full.

The decision would have to be made bearing in mind a number of other factors – some good, some bad. On the positive side – in July, an unknown donor, who was not a church member, had promised £25,000 to the building fund if it was matched by fresh giving. The offer came at a critical moment. July saw a slump in monthly giving back to the £4,000 mark from the £24,000 level of May and June. On the negative side, the possible quick sale of the Waldegrave Hall had fallen through again and there were pessimistic forecasts about the government's Land Development Tax, thought to be coming into effect in 1976.

The church had had to face crises in the past, and God had kept hidden his way forward until the step of faith had been taken. Was this to happen again?

Little could be done during August when many members – students, teachers and families with young children – were away on holiday. A special meeting of the church family was called for the evening of 2 September. It was well attended, and for Michael Baughen and many others, became a moving occasion.

He made it his task to apprise the church of the full consequences of not signing the contract now with Harrison and Harrison for the restructured organ: the new church would probably have to open without it at all, or possibly with an unsatisfactory alternative electronic instrument costing something like £17,000 but guaranteed, incredibly, for only fifteen years; the west gallery of the newly opened church would be cluttered with organ pipes awaiting reassembly; lastly there was a strong possibility that without a decent organ the BBC would not wish to continue its contract with the church – an important source of income.

'Factually, and humanly speaking, we were in a very difficult position,' Michael Baughen recalled, 'for we had no idea where that extra £50,000 for the organ was coming

79

from, and we were still only about half way in our giving.'
(The fund stood in fact at about £240,000.) 'The verse that
stood out for me was 1 Kings 8:56 "not one word has failed
of his good promises . . . " and I shared this with the meeting.
God had guided me to this verse and as I had meditated on
it I saw that the project was not a matter simply of *our*
integrity of word to the builders, but overall the integrity of
God's word to us. Had he not led us so clearly? Was not his
word to be trusted? It eased the burden to see the matter in
these terms.' Alongside that, he could also share the good
news, received in the post that very morning, that the Billy
Graham Evangelistic Trust in the United States was giving
£11,000 from a special projects fund.

So the mood of the meeting was not despondent, and
though Michael did not take a vote on the matter, allowing
time instead for prayer and discussion, it was very clear
that the members did not want to open the new building
without the old organ restored to its splendour, leading the
singing as it had done so often in the past.

To confirm this, many people came up to Michael afterwards telling him that they were prepared to sell their most
treasured possessions to ensure the money was there to pay
for the organ. 'It was a real help to feel people were truly
committed to the idea,' he commented. 'For there were
genuine problems in our minds about spending all that
money when the needs of the Third World are so great. But
when you've got a Rolls Royce of an organ (already worth
a lot of money) do you just let it rot – or do you treat it like
a Rolls Royce?'

Two days later, when the council confirmed that decision
and the contract was duly signed, they were told that the
renovated organ would be one of the finest in the country.
Colin Goulden, one of All Souls' organists, and soon to
become President of the Organ Club of Great Britain, was
to confer with Noel Tredinnick and Harrisons to create a
scheme for the new instrument – which included the adding
of a fourth manual and a second console – best suited to its
future use: leading the congregational singing; accompany-

ing choir and orchestra; supporting smaller choirs in the chancel such as were used in the BBC's Daily Service; and as a solo instrument in its own right.

These were the facts of the scheme – but God's encouragement to the step taken was to be breathtaking.

The beginning of the final 'Year of Giving' (October 1975–76) was to be historic for a number of reasons. First it was marked by the official 'retirement' of the Rev. John R. W. Stott, MA, QHC, as Rector of All Souls, on 29 September 1975, the twenty-fifth anniversary of his institution. His close link with All Souls was to remain in his new role of Rector Emeritus but he would be absent from the parish for longer periods in the future, writing books, preaching and teaching abroad. The church would be rectorless for a period of five to six weeks only; on 7 November 1975 Michael Baughen was to be instituted by the Bishop of London, the Rt Rev. Gerald Ellison.

John Stott's role as 'All Souls Ambassador at Large' (as Crusade magazine dubbed him) had already begun to reap unexpected rewards when many gifts to the building fund came from overseas. Australian and American friends in particular were in the forefront of this generosity. On his very next trip to the States that autumn, John Stott was able to distribute about six hundred appeal brochures in three major cities and a further fifty in New York.

His stay in the latter city proved more fruitful than he or anyone else could have imagined. He had been invited there to speak at the Annual Episcopal Renewal Conference and a friend had suggested that instead of booking into a hotel he should stay with a Mrs Caroline Lynch, who was a widow with a large Park Avenue flat. For her part, Mrs Lynch asked if she could invite some friends in to meet her guest and hear all about the exciting project at All Souls. So after supper one evening, John Stott had the opportunity of showing his slides and talking about the plans for the church.

Not only the guests but also his hostess expressed great interest in the project – and Mrs Lynch was a woman of her word. She crossed the Atlantic to see the building (now

6

being excavated) for herself in late October. Soon came the fantastic news that she wished to donate $100,000 (about £50,000) to the fund! She preferred to give it towards something specific – had John Stott any suggestions?

In his reply John Stott listed three items in this order: the new organ, a proposed counselling centre to be built under the portico; the new refectory. Back came Mrs Lynch's preference. She wished the money to pay for the new organ – 'in gratitude for my three children – Eddie, Virginia and Case'.

It was an incredible answer to the prayers of that September meeting, when the church had committed itself to raising the money for the organ come what may. God's answer, once again, had been withheld until the church had been prepared to go out in faith. 'We didn't realise it, but the wells of Elim were just around the corner,' was Michael Baughen's comment. 'But that is what made our pilgrimage of faith so exciting. Despite the problems, instead of saying "Horrors! We can't do that . . . the waters are bitter, let's go back to Egypt", the people still pressed on.'

> *I miss greatly the teaching of the
> services at All Souls – sometimes here
> I find it hard to remember that God is
> a loving God in spite of all the suffer-
> ing.*
>
> A donor from Vietnam

Gifts to All Souls Building Fund from overseas invariably brought welcome news from friends and former members and expressions of gratitude for the ministry of All Souls and of John Stott and Michael Baughen.

An American wife and mother sent with her donation a note saying, 'My thanks to the All Souls staff and fellowship which played a part both directly and indirectly in bringing our family to England for my husband to study for the ministry.'

Another American wrote, 'By strange coincidence the Gospel read today at our local parish church recounted our Lord's meeting with the two disciples on the road to Emmaus. In April 1971 I was profoundly influenced by a sermon based on this portion of Holy Scripture to which I listened at All Souls, so, in a sense, you may regard this contribution as a thanksgiving.'

Dr Billy Graham in a letter to Michael Baughen added, 'I am deeply grateful for what All Souls has meant to me during these many years.'

Australian generosity might not have resulted in gifts of the same magnitude as Mrs Lynch's, but the longstanding

83

warm friendship between John Stott and the Sydney diocese, in particular, meant that Archbishop Marcus Loane gladly sponsored the project publicly in the brochure and Bishop Donald Cameron became the fund's honorary treasurer in Australia. Furthermore, the mother of an Australian member kindly acted as 'agent', sending out brochures from her home in Melbourne.

In letters from Australia, too, former members were thrilled to be involved in the project from so far away.

'Thank you for the opportunity to share with you in your present need,' one wrote. 'After seven months at home here, I am still most thankful for the enriching two years that I was able to spend with you.'

Another gladly gave from her first earnings after returning home and wrote, 'It is with joy and thanksgiving, and not just a little awe, that I enclose this cheque for the building fund, which I have saved in just seven weeks, since I began working again after a break of two and a half years without a salary or regular income.'

Some Australian gifts came from people who knew All Souls only slightly. 'Last year I spent some time flitting in and out of All Souls, whenever I was in London, and developed a real love for the church,' one wrote; while another explained, 'We have followed with interest, via your magazine, news of the project, and rejoice with you that the work has now begun ...'

Possibly this letter from an Australian clergyman sums up the deep sense of indebtedness that many others felt. 'John Stott has been of more blessing and help to me in my ministry through his preaching and writing than any other person. It was a thrill to be with you for two Sundays last August. I am writing to let you know that you should be receiving a gift from my previous parishioners. They have allocated half of their annual gift day to your building project.'

The worldwide appeal drew a response from many other countries also. From South Africa came another generous gift from a parish church, this time in Durban. The vicar wrote, 'We should like to share with you in your worthy project both as an act of fellowship and also because so many of our members have benefitted through the work of All Souls . . . The good wishes of the whole of our congregation here is sent with this love gift to the congregation of All Souls.'

A Rhodesian doctor in Bulawayo, recently converted along with his wife, felt he wanted to contribute to the building fund at All Souls where his daughter was a member.

In New Zealand the parents of a former member, despite problems in the family, 'couldn't resist the urge to help just a little in your big project'.

A friend of John Stott in Vancouver, Canada, wrote, 'I am delighted to share in the cost of the building project as it is one small way of saying "thank you" for all that you have brought to me over the years in audible ministry, in person and on tape, and in written ministry through many books and articles.'

Usually, however, Michael Baughan and John Stott were linked in the expressions of gratitude. A donor from Barbados added, 'I should just mention that I received much blessing on various trips to England through your books, Keswick ministries and, of course, at services at All Souls. Thank you both very much indeed.'

As a complete contrast, another friend wrote to both men from war-ravaged Vietnam: 'I am following the progress of the building project with much interest and I feel I want to help you all. Living here, money has come to mean even less to me than it did back in London, but I'm afraid these are all the pounds I have with me here, but I guess every little helps. Although I have fellowship with some fine Christians here, I miss greatly the teaching of the services at All Souls – sometimes here I find it hard to remember that God is a loving God in spite of all the suffering that goes on.'

The giving to the fund by missionaries abroad never failed to challenge the fellowship. From Northern Sumatra, Indonesia, an O.M.F. missionary wrote: 'This is the second part of my two instalment gift and I am very thankful that, because of his goodness and care for us over the past years, I am in a position to add an extra £25 to the originally promised £100 to help the church counter the terrific inflation over the past year. May the new church be speedily completed and be used by the Lord to make his name known to thousands.'

Another All Souls missionary with the O.M.F. summed up the feelings of many others about the fund when she wrote, 'I am so grateful to God for his abundance that enables me to give and not just receive ... On the eve of sailing back to the Far East I rejoice that I can share in a new way in fellowship and thanksgiving with you in being able to send the enclosed cheque.'

Serving God in Africa, an All Souls missionary couple sent their gift and commented, 'The missionary giving of the Church is not a one way thing but a mutual sharing of prayer and financial support.'

Mutual sharing was indeed the keynote of the response to the fund in Britain and from many many other countries. Each gift received by post was acknowledged personally wherever possible, involving much extra work not only for John Stott and Michael Baughen, but for their two secretaries Frances Whitehead and Di Wheeler and the Church Administrator, Grace Jackson.

Mutual sharing was the keynote, also, when it came to a fitting tribute to the twenty-five year ministry of John Stott, who refused to accept any personal gift. The suggestion that it should be in the form of some part of the new All Souls did meet with his approval. So what could be more appropriate than a new pulpit, suitably inscribed, as a mark of the church's gratitude for his dedicated ministry? The pulpit fund was duly launched in the autumn and proved its value to the full when the generous response paid for the new communion table also.

At the suggestion of Archdeacon Sam Woodhouse and Robert Potter, Michael and Myrtle Baughen had been to see the sculpture of Geoffrey Clarke in Chichester Cathedral. They liked what they saw and it was Clarke who was asked to submit designs and estimates for the new pulpit in All Souls. He had a very difficult task, for the specification was that it should be movable, and not obscure the rest of the chancel, especially the communion table, yet the preacher must be visible to the whole congregation. His unusual winged design submitted in December was accepted by the P.C.C. and subsequently by the Diocesan Advisory Committee.

Historic events still continued to mark this the final year of the project. November saw two of especial significance. On All Souls Gift Day – 3 November – the builders kindly opened up the newly excavated site and, for the first time ever, the congregation saw Nash's superb arched foundations and could stand on the bare boards, laid where the basement floor would be.

'Fantastic' was the general consensus of opinion as people gazed around the now hollow shell of the church. The eye could travel down from the dim ceiling, the towering columns, the boarded up gallery fronts, to the line marking, where the church floor had been thirteen feet above. Then, best of all, they could see and touch the original brickwork of the curved inverted arches. Having been hidden for 150 years they had taken almost two years since their discovery to expose. There was a sense of awe at what God had done.

'Fantastic' was also Michael Baughen's comment – this time about the workmen's speed and expertise in excavating the building with few delays, removing the 6,000 cubic yards of earth in five weeks, a week ahead of schedule. Fixed in Michael's memory was the sight of the man driving the earth moving equipment. Once the basement floor had been dug out to its full depth of thirteen feet, to remove the earth he had to drive his loaded machine at some speed up a very steep ramp. Then without daring to pause he had to aim it straight for the narrow specially made opening in the side wall scarcely wider than his bulldozer. 'In fact I think he only tipped his load over in the wrong place once. He did trip after trip so fast you could not help being fascinated by his speed and accuracy,' Michael commented.

Winching the long steel beams through that narrow side entrance was yet another traumatic moment. It was essential (on police orders) that the nine beams for the new church floor be delivered on a Sunday to avoid weekday traffic – because a tall motorised crane had to be used to lift them one by one from their articulated lorry parked in Langham Place. Then each was slowly and carefully slotted into the small entrance. The task of guiding them once inside the church was not simple either, for their length made their manoeuverability very difficult. The church's film maker, David Nunn, had a field day with his cine camera, focusing on the delicacy of the whole operation as one man guided the crane driver who had to work 'blind' when lowering the beam to just the right level before it could proceed into the building. Watching this slow tortuous procedure made some people realise how much easier the whole job would have been if the church had been demolished and the builders had started from scratch.

The other historic moment of that November was Michael Baughen's institution and induction as Rector of All Souls on 7 November at St Peter's, Vere Street. To any Anglican who knows his rubric, the induction of a new incumbent usually takes place in his new church. For fairly obvious reasons, in Michael's case this was impossible!

But the service was nonetheless meaningful to all concerned. Archdeacon Samuel Woodhouse for one, was to remember vividly the moment when, after the institution at St Peter's, he and the Bishop of London and Michael Baughen had to disappear quickly to drive across to the deserted dark All Souls. The brief induction service followed under the portico, Michael Baughen laying his hand upon the front door of the empty gutted building to take possession of it . . . Then the door opened and all that could be seen beyond was 'a colossal hole. We could see right to the bottom, where the hall was to be'.

The Bishop, for his part, found the occasion almost unique and said so in his address. He was instituting the new rector in a building that was not his parish church. He was doing so in the presence of the previous rector, and there was no point in introducing the new rector to his new congregation; they had known each other for five years!

Michael Baughen had tried hard to play down the institution but the All Souls family were in no mood to co-operate. The occasion, they felt, was a fitting sequel to five years inspiring leadership – and the love and affection of many was expressed that evening to the new rector and his family.

11 The Pressure is On

Do all British workmen work like this?

Overseas visitor to the site

'If you were given a £600,000 church complex in the centre of London, in the Britain of 1976, with no pre-supposed programme whatsoever, how would you use that complex? What are the priorities?'

These were some of the questions facing the two church Day Conferences held in January 1976. In all 250 members attended the conferences at Oak Hill College, Southgate, and, divided into twenty-one groups, they studied the questions in some detail under such headings as evangelism, organisations, fellowship, teaching and training, and use of buildings. The leader of each group passed on to Michael Baughen a report of the discussions and eventually a compilation of the varied suggestions and comments was drawn up by him to help plan the best use for the new facilities.

In the light of future events, two suggestions proved of significant value: first – a general feeling against a mission to mark the opening on 2 November, with a preference for a 'blitz' on the parish, visiting every home to invite the residents to see the new building; second – a warm approval for some kind of welcome or reception desk manned whenever the building was open.

In some respects the conference reports seemed a bit idealistic, because many church members had difficulty in relating to the new building's limitations. They had seen only plans and drawings which not all of them understood. If

90

some suggestions were wildly optimistic, the general feeling was one of eager anticipation!

But the grim realities of the financial situation soon dispelled any euphoria in the air. Despite a week-long advertising campaign in September 1975, backed by special prayer, the Waldegrave Hall was still unsold in January 1976 and the agent was not hopeful of any sale in the present economic crisis.

On the positive side, the Trustees had been able, at last to pay into the fund the promised £100,000. Other special events like the November Gift Day (£14,800) and the Christmas Market (£1,005), had added impetus to the steady giving so that by 1 February, the half way point in the eighteen-month project, the fund had reached a total of about £411,000 with expenditure standing at around £212,000.

With only nine months to go to sell the Waldegrave Hall in time to give the other £200,000, the Trustees began to feel the pressure of time was against them. In January, after John Stott had met with them, they asked All Souls church council to nominate a second estate agent. This was done, noting the extra cost involved. But the general feeling was that a fresh mind on the job would be a good thing.

The progress in selling the hall might be very slow but that was not true of the preparations for equipping and furnishing the new building. A further happy factor in Robert Potter's appointment as architect was the involvement of his wife, Margaret, as design consultant for choosing colour schemes, fabrics, fittings and other decor. This family team became the central pivot of all the planning in this area.

It was right back on Decision Day in April 1975, in fact, that the Potters asked that study groups be set up to look at the various and varying needs of the new building. In the end, three sub-committees were appointed, liaising where necessary with stockists, manufacturers and, of course, with Robert and Margaret.

The Kitchen Study Group, in collaboration with James

Stott and Company of Oldham, catering equipment manufacturers, drew up a design layout and negotiated the ordering of the necessary materials for the big refectory kitchen by October 1975.

The Electricity and Electronics group had such a wide brief that they found it necessary to subdivide to look at future needs for lighting, public address systems and TV links. They also had to keep in close touch with the BBC engineers to ascertain that the correct equipment for them was installed. Eventually a professional co-ordinator was appointed and by mid-November the wiring and siting of equipment was in hand, while in December Robert Potter was able to agree the trunk routes for the electricity supply.

The Decoration and Furnishing Study Group took themselves off to Chelmsford, Essex, to see the latest ideas in church decor and furniture at Christchurch there, then set themselves the task of deciding what were the furnishing needs of the various areas in the new building. Then they prepared to discuss the details with the Potters.

Chairs were one preoccupation at this time. Not for the new hall, because it had been agreed that stackable chairs be used there and in the refectory. But chairs for the church and seating for the gallery were a major consideration. Visits to see samples in use at St Paul's Cathedral and the Millmead Centre, Guildford, were made before the end of 1975 and in January 1976 four possibilities were shown to the council who did not like any of them.

Although members in fact did not like the idea of losing all the pews, after much discussion it was decided to have radial seating throughout the ground floor (made up of rows of linked chairs of a type still to be chosen) and fixed bench seating in the galleries similar to the type seen at Guildford.

February finally became the month of the chair, with an 'extraordinary' (in more ways than one) council meeting held on the stage of the hall used for prayer meeting, to try out no less than twenty-five different chairs. After much standing, sitting and discussion about appearance, the choice

92

was narrowed down to three. These were submitted to Robert Potter, who chose one but decided to adapt it to All Souls's particular need – a wide shelf at the rear for RSV Bible, two hymnbooks, and service cards. The chair thereafter became known as the 'Langham chair' after its new home.

By the end of May considerable progress had also been made with carpets and colourings. It was far cheaper to use carpet than wood for floor coverings, and a tough grey-green one was chosen for the church, with the exception of the chancel area which was to be laid in wood on the advice of the BBC to improve the acoustics.

The new Waldegrave Hall in the basement was to have dark brown carpet tiles while at the foot of the delicately curved staircase from the rotunda, where the visitor would first glimpse the hall, an attractive circular vestibule incorporated a purple carpet. Within the hall the stackable chairs were to be bright orange, matching the heavy-weave orange and brown full-length curtains to divide the room. The refectory windows were to have green curtains, contrasting with bright yellow chairs and ceramic tiles on the floor.

By far the most important pieces of furniture, those for the chancel, depended for their acceptance not only on the church council but also upon the approval of the Diocesan Advisory Committee to whom many applications were made during the whole project. The most important item for which approval was sought was Geoffrey Clarke's ultra-modern design for the new pulpit. However, when the D.A.C. gave their assent, they insisted that the communion table and font be in the same design family.

Previous reservations about the cost of these two items (as estimated by the sculptor) had to be reconsidered in the light of this diocesan pressure – and the lack of time left for the commissions to be completed. Surely, one council member pointed out, these objects were not going to be merely functional – they were to service the Word and the Sacrament. This was what the church was all about. Spending this extra money was well worthwhile when judged in

93

that light. The council agreed, and asked to see designs for the communion table and font as soon as Geoffrey Clarke could prepare them. By the time the drawings were to hand, the decision to proceed was made a great deal easier by the knowledge that the John Stott pulpit fund had overflowed its coffers and would help towards paying for these two items.

The need to balance the laudable desire for the best possible quality against undue extravagance, brought its own particular pressures; the chancel furniture being but one case in point. 'The larger items were not necessarily chosen for their excellence if they were more expensive,' Michael Baughen explained. 'We tried to balance the best with the cheapest – making intelligent decisions. Where we have had expensive items – the ashwood in the refectory, for instance, or the chancel furniture, we say "Come back in twenty or thirty years' time and these things will still be in excellent condition. They have been put in to last."

'We could have saved money, too, by putting back the old wooden pews. But I believe we are right to match the new design of the church with new furniture. We are trying to serve the gospel, and I don't think it is served by Victorian hard wooden pews!'

Michael Baughen listed certain expensive additions to the final bill which had not been expected – such as the lift to the basement required for use by the disabled and elderly. To give both the hall and the church a welcoming openness, glass doors had been planned at the rear of each so that the visitor could see straight in. But to meet with the requirements laid down by the fire prevention officer from the Westminster planning department, extra doors combining reinforced glass and wood had to be installed. Expensive metal ventilation cowlings in the kitchen and the hardwood chancel floor were other examples of extras that the church had not planned to include.

In fact, coping with the demands of officialdom caused a number of problems from the start. Naturally the local authorities were concerned that the building should be safe for public use, but some of the regulations which seemed more suited to theatres and cinemas than a church, were difficult to comply with.

One particular bone of contention was the flooring in chipboard of the re-raked galleries. The new floor had barely been completed when the District Surveyor rang up to say that in the London building regulations chipboard was prohibited for weight-bearing. Yet, as Michael Baughen pointed out, the plans for the gallery floors had been with the planning department well in advance; why had they only been informed of this now?

Meanwhile the builders had pressures of their own with which to cope. The excavation might have been swift and easy, but not so the drilling through of the foundations. It was essential that the base of the inverted arches be considerably strengthened before the weight of the other steel beams could be hung on them. Each wall had to have along either side of it, a huge reinforced concrete beam tightly clamped to its neighbour on the other side of the very thick brickwork.

In order to pass the necessary 200 steel rods through the wall, 200 holes had to be drilled. With compressors the drilling would have taken a few days – but then came the hitch. The engineers refused to let them be used, concerned that the pounding the building above might take in the process would considerably weaken it.

No compressors meant using ordinary power drills which broke under the strain of the tough work causing further frustrating delays. The job took weeks instead of a few days.

Much later in the rebuilding, when the organ builders moved on to the site to begin reconstructing the new organ, a further delay occurred. The old organ loft floor in the west gallery, on close inspection, was showing signs of weakness and would not take the extra weight of the new instrument. Some fairly intricate engineering and building work was necessary before, seven weeks behind schedule, work on the organ could begin.

In general, however, the delays did not affect the final

result, and did not manage to dampen the enthusiasm and humour of the workmen on the site, causing one admiring overseas visitor to ask, 'Do all British workmen work like this?'

On other occasions, mutual admiration flowed in the other direction. The congregation was due to visit the site one Sunday morning, and arrived to find a huge blackboard at the entrance bearing a beautifully chalked message from the builders thanking Michael Baughen, John Stott and the All Souls family for all their help and interest.

Michael Baughen saw at close quarters in the fortnightly site meetings just how the tone of the work schedule was set by Robert Potter, who began each meeting with prayer, and by the care and concern of the builder's site agent, John Gallagher.

The high standards achieved by the contractors throughout earned them such comments as 'wonderful attention to detail', 'high quality of craftsmanship', 'sheer hard work' and 'marvellous co-operation' in the special brochure published for the opening.

But before that, there were six months of mounting tension and prayerful effort as the church tried to match the ever-rising estimate for the final job, with more and more giving.

Compared with 1974's monthly average income of £4,000 or less, the 1976 figures were gratifying: April £11,900, May £10,800, June £12,900 and July £10,900. By mid-June the fund passed the half million mark, with continuing careful investment and the recovery of tax from covenant gifts.

On the negative side, though, the project expenditure by this stage had risen to £371,000 and – ghastly thought – the final sum was now expected to be about £714,000. The yawning gap of £343,000 still remained to challenge the church to pray, especially for the sale of the Waldegrave Hall.

For the Trustees, the appointment of a second agent had proved a turning point. There seemed to be more optimism and activity and in May they met to decide their policy for the final months when every effort to sell the hall urgently before November must be made. Decision Day for them was set as 24 August 1976. If the hall was not sold for the right price by then they would consider letting it to the client who had already enquired about this possibility. But this alternative was far less satisfactory for all concerned than a sale, because the final income would not be to hand for some considerable time.

The fortnightly prayer gatherings, the fellowship groups, the Thursday morning project prayer times and each individual member – all tried to be faithful in praying for the sale of the hall. But it taxed many people's faith to believe that after two and a half years and no answer, God was ever going to meet this particular need.

Was God calling the church to prove him in raising a further £200,000? This was the thought in many minds – though few doubted now that God's purpose was being fulfilled in the wonderful transformation taking place behind the hoardings surrounding the famous portico. Except possibly the unbalanced person who kept defacing the posters pasted on them, claiming that the builders and clergy were vandals because there had always been a basement hall under the church!

12   The Final Heave

This is not the end, you know. This is only the beginning.

Church member

The finale of the All Souls Building Project was, to say the least, suitably exciting for all concerned. God had already revealed his miraculous power in amazing ways with the overcoming of various 'giants' in the path of its launching and the preparation of the members to enter into the faith-pilgrimage. His guidance had been clearly seen in the appointment of Robert Potter, the decision to excavate beneath All Souls, finding the lovely arches, and finally in the fantastic giving to the fund alongside the excellent progress made by the builders whose work was of such high quality. What more could there be, over and above all that the church could ask or think, for God to do? Ah yes, find a buyer for the Waldegrave Hall.

Almost imperceptibly the impossible happened unheralded and unsung. On 23 August, the day before the Waldegrave Hall Trustees' decision day, the hall was sold! It being the end of August, many people were away. Indeed, Michael Baughen and his family had only just returned from a well-earned break. The prayer of the church family had been that he might return to find the hall sold. As it happened, God chose to complete the sale on the Monday of the next week, when he was back at his desk.

John Stott and the other Trustees, only too aware of the deadline they had set, were doing all in their power to expedite matters, rushing vital documents by hand to addresses outside London in order to have them signed and exchanged by 24 August.

Thus the 'extraordinary' meeting of the church council called for the evening of that date, began on a high note of praise and amazed rejoicing as Michael Baughen announced that the hall had been sold. God's answer to the prayers of hundreds had been withheld almost until the last: a rebuke to the little faith of some; a seal on the firm conviction of others.

For Michael himself the signing and exchange of documents was coupled with another small miracle. The sale of the hall included one snag. The purchaser wanted time for completion and instead of the money being immediately available, £150,000 would not be paid until the end of the year, *after* All Souls completion date. As contractors' bills would have to be paid before then, it was clear that much of this amount would be needed before it was received.

Michael felt that this matter ought to be sorted out before facing the Council that evening. He knew there was already provision for a £100,000 bridging loan from the Bank if required. But now a £50,000 extension was essential and normally such extensions took time to be processed through the bank's official channels.

Yet once again God had prepared the way. Long before his holiday, Michael had been invited to have lunch with the directors of the local bank – a date changed several times and eventually agreed for 25 August, the very day of the church council meeting. Michael had wanted to change it again but felt unable to do so. Now, many weeks after first arranging the date, it proved providential. The lunch invitation, it transpired, was in order to ask him whether the bank's carol service could be held at the new All Souls, and in the informal atmosphere Michael felt able to raise the question of the extra £50,000 loan provision. It was granted without hesitation. When Michael met the council that evening, even that detail had been worked out and settled.

The bank loan was definitely reassuring. But Michael's

vision and hope was that the new All Souls should open on All Souls Day, 2 November, without having to use the loan, and not owing a penny. This was the aim of the final weeks of prayer and giving, stimulated by the Appeal Letter sent out by Michael Baughen and John Stott and the church-wardens on 2 September to the extended church family:

'Now we come to the final two months. The work is close to schedule and all should be ready for 2 November. On the financial side we are 92 per cent of the way! It is less than two years since the Parochial Church Council took the great decision to go ahead to "tender" stage. At that time (12 October 1974) the total costing they had to face for the project, the rebuilding of the organ and the reno-vation of St Peter's, was £750,000. It was a step of faith not taken lightly! Now at this moment we have received in cash or firm commitment £705,000 towards the revised overall figure of £765,000. It is humbling, thrilling and amazing! The "gap" remaining is approximately £60,000 (8 per cent of the overall target). This is still a very large sum of money but we now set our hearts and prayers to see it in hand by 2 November so that, as we have prayed all along, we may open the new building free of debt to the Lord's glory.'

Right until the last minute small miracles of timing occurred. Just when the expenditure threatened to overtake the income one week-end in September, with a £51,000 bill due for payment for which the fund lacked £5,500, a cheque for £5,600 was placed in the offering plate for the building project. The donor was quite unaware of the unusual need.

A special evening of prayer on the Tuesday before the Gift Day, Sunday 26 September, set the tone of expectancy and thanksgiving. The services morning and evening on the day itself were packed long before they began, and the sides-men could scarcely cope with the offering. Michael Baughen reminded the church that their praise and thanksgiving must have an element of awe about it. His words proved timely – for a sense of wonder overcame the family gathered after the evening service to hear the result of the appeal. The total of the final heave in just twenty-four days was an incredible £54,000 – only £6,000 more was needed by the beginning of November! The atmosphere was one of amazement and emotion, Michael himself having difficulty in speaking when he came to make the much-anticipated announcement and write the figures on the overhead projector for all to see.

But the position was clear. Of the £765,000 needed, £759,000 was now in hand. On that Gift Day alone the giving had totalled £31,000 from people who had already given a great deal. The joyous relief of knowing that the battle was all but won gave the day a special meaning for all present.

Andrew Scott who handled the cheques and banked the fund money, never ceased to marvel at the steady giving throughout the project. The majority of the money came, not from a few wealthy benefactors, but from many members of the church family who decided to tithe or more than tithe their income. Many small gifts flowed in; added to them came regular amounts of say £10, £20, £30, given by the same people. But many preferred to hold back and give a lump sum on special days – £100, £200, £1,000. In the end, the congregation alone without outside help, had been responsible for giving about £450,000 in two years – an incredible achievement!

The major stimulus to the giving had definitely been the publication of the Appeal Brochure in February 1975 as revealed in the rising monthly income that followed: March £20,000, April £40,000, May and June around £24,500 each. It was clear, too, that the quantity surveyors and Robert Potter had been remarkably accurate in their costings and forecasts of expenditure needs by certain dates, thus enabling realistic targets to be set in plenty of time.

For most of the project, therefore, the two lines on Andrew's graph of accumulated income and expenditure ran almost parallel – with about £100,000 always in hand, invested on the advice of brokers in short term investments.

It should also be remembered that during the project All Souls had other financial responsibilities. One was the support of the church's thirty missionaries. It had been hoped that there would be no drop back in giving at the annual Missionary Gift Day but in 1975 money did appear to have been deflected. The day's total was £1,000 below that of the previous year. But in 1976 matters righted themselves with £6,700 being given, £2,000 more than 1975.

Another financial responsibility was the general fund out of which staff salaries, administration and other expenses were paid. The church treasurer admitted that these funds appeared to have suffered most during the project. Offerings fell in any case once the church moved to St Peter's and by the end of 1975 the general church accounts were in the red. He was very confident that back in All Souls matters would sort themselves out again.

But before that moment, and to celebrate the opening of the new building free of debt as the whole church family had hoped, the offerings on 2 November were dedicated to helping world need.

Many church members were convinced, too, that once the project was over the giving of the church family would be different anyway. The project had proved how much and how sacrificially they had been able to give – and what a joy it had been to do so. The challenge for the future surely was 'If I could give all that money then, why am I not prepared to go on giving generously now?'

All the people who testified publicly at the final service in St Peter's of what the project had meant to them, spoke of God's faithfulness in enabling them to give – more than they had ever dreamed. Most of them had taken Bishop Alf Stanway's suggestion to heart – 'think of a figure then double it' – and found that God was no man's debtor. 'Each time I gave – a cheque arrived unexpectedly,' said one. Another spoke of proving Proverbs 11.24: 'One man gives freely yet grows all the richer,' and of being enabled to double and double again the amount given to the fund. A married couple with a wife at home with their baby, decided to forgo a much-needed gas cooker in order to give more. 'Yet money just kept pouring in – over and above what we needed – and we got our new cooker also.' It had been a time of personal miracles, of seeing God take the few loaves and fishes and make them into something wonderful to his glory.

The sense of a new unity among the family was very evident in those final weeks of giving and preparation for the opening. As Michael Baughen expressed it, 'When you've wept together and rejoiced together, you have a new kind of appreciation of each other.' For one member of the staff team, John Aldis, it had been a privilege to be part of the project, for he had been shown afresh that 'the living God of power, the God of might, this God is our God.' For another staff member, an American soon to return to the States, the experience had given him an insight into the gifts of leadership needed for such a faith project. He had watched Michael Baughen, in particular, setting the church on its course, trying not to push too hard on the one hand, and not to hold back too much on the other; yet making Jesus Christ and his glory central to the whole.

What had the experience meant to Michael Baughen himself? His mind could go back to several heart-stopping occasions when every signal seemed to be flashing red. Yet the feeling was that God left the church with no alternative but to move on into the unknown. 'This is what I call an Abraham or Moses experience. You are thrown on God without knowing how things will work out. The God of the impossible then shows himself. So he has again for us. Hallelujah!'

Michael was also aware that to some people All Souls appeared a rich church, with many influential professional people in its membership. Perhaps raising such a large sum of money had not been such an achievement after all? He agreed that in comparison with his previous parish in Manchester, All Souls could be called 'rich'. More people had monthly salaries and bank accounts, and there were more single people in membership who, though highly taxed, had fewer financial commitments. But the timing of the appeal had also been in the project's favour. From 1974 onwards, many members, particularly in the medical and para-medical professions received back-dated pay awards, and gladly gave all or some of these to the fund. It mattered not, though, how much or how little was given – it was God who had honoured and blessed the whole.

If this sounded like spiritualising the matter, Michael Baughen agreed he was never averse to supplying the church family with some concrete financial guidelines: pledges, costings, a target for which to aim. 'I believe that alongside prayer and faith it is useful to have figures to help people think out what they can give. You have to stretch people's ideas.'

It was a happy bonus therefore for the All Souls building project, that the man whom John Stott invited to take charge of the church had not only been through a building project in his previous parish, but also had a facility with figures. Mathematics had been Michael's best subject at school and he went into banking for two years after leaving. Undeterred by doing National Service, he continued to study for his banking exams, though he only returned to the bank for a year before he entered training for the ministry. But his gift for sorting out and organising figures did not desert him. At All Souls it had been an undeniable asset. In the crucial decision-making stages of the fund he was able to present the financial facts in a way which was understood by even the least mathematically-inclined members of his council.

All in all, God had used a multitude of talents – great and small – to bring to pass the rebuilding and refurbishing of All Souls. Who would have thought that an archdeacon who would have loved to be an architect, and a vicar who nearly went into banking, would have had such a profound effect on one London church!

The question, as the opening approached, was, 'Is the church ready to take up and shoulder the challenge of the new buildings?' One member summed it up by saying, 'This is not the end, you know. This is only the beginning.'

13 Onward Christian Soldiers!

We cannot tell all you have planned
*   and purposed, Lord,*
To use this church renewed to spread
*   your word,*
And so we pray that we may be
*   obedient*
To do your will whatever that may be.

Michael Baughen

The final month before the opening flew past. The £6,000
needed to exceed the total was in hand by 18 October. But
there was no danger of any excess in the fund being wasted,
for final bills, affected by inflation, were not due until the
middle of 1977.

Best of all, the hoarding around the church came down
and, as Opening Day drew near, excitement mounted at
seeing the new building almost completed. Work went on
literally day and night to make certain that by 2 November
the church and hall were presentable to public gaze. Members took time off work to help clean and prepare the building. The Saturday before, a valiant team tackled the filthy
curved portico steps unwashed since goodness knows when.
Scrubbing them was such mucky work that the BBC pro-
ducer of a programme due to highlight people doing dirty
jobs, invited them to attend the recording the next week.
When the team duly went along to the studio they found
their 'colleagues' were sewage workers and window cleaners!

The night before the opening the church council gathered
in the new Waldegrave Hall (still not completely clear of

builders' rubbish), and – almost too overwhelmed by everything – tried to voice their thanks to God. Upstairs in the church rows of chairs still had to be put in place, and service books sorted out. In every corner, sweeping, tidying and clearing up was in progress. The only major event that had dampened the proceedings, occurred as the electricians completed the hanging of the beautiful Potter-designed chandeliers. The last one to be wound slowly up to the high ceiling from floor level was at the front, over the chancel. Suddenly, without warning, it fell from a considerable height to crash on the newly polished afromosia chancel flooring, breaking some of the glass globes, and scoring marks in the wood.

The workmen were horrified – there were no spare glass lampshades and the floor, even when re-sanded and polished, still showed the scars of the accident. But with a further session of chandelier hanging, globes from the rear of the church replaced those at the front and no one was any the wiser.

For many people the climax of the whole Opening and Re-dedication Service, for which queues formed hours beforehand, was the final hymn – 'Onward, Christian Soldiers'. With full organ, orchestra and brass, clergy, choir and the 1,500-plus congregation (which included nearly 300 builders and technicians who had helped to construct the new facilities, most of whom knew the chorus if not the hymn) played and sang as they never had before. Particularly moving was the sight of the church hierarchy, represented by the Bishop, and the Archdeacon of London, at the head of a procession which included Robert Potter, and members of the various firms involved, marching down the widened centre aisle to the words:

> Crowns and thrones may perish
> Kingdoms rise and wane;
> But the church of Jesus
> Constant will remain;
> Gates of hell can never

'Gainst that church prevail;
We have Christ's own promise,
And that cannot fail ...

Before the Opening a press conference had been held
and it was gratifying to see, during the following weeks, the
excellent coverage the new church received. *The Times,
Daily Telegraph, Evening Standard, Marylebone Mercury*
– to name but a few papers along with radio and TV, took
the trouble to give time or space to the new facilities. The
BBC's World Service went one better with a half-hour
broadcast of the actual Rededication. Many friends of the
church abroad, wrote to say what a thrill it was to hear this
in such far away places as Libya, Uganda and even Australia.

But at All Souls, 'Onward, Christian Soldiers' was certainly the motto for the first week back in the church. No
sooner had the building been opened, than it was closed
again while the parish 'blitz' took place. All the courage
and energy of the congregation was needed for the next
three nights (Wednesday, Thursday and Friday) as they
visited every home with special invitation cards asking the
residents in to see 'your parish church' on the following
Saturday from 11 a.m. until 6 p.m.

Many members of the church family who made the effort
to help in the visiting, admitted they had never done anything like it before. But by God's grace they were going to do
it now. All were frankly frightened, yet enthused by this
golden opportunity to make the church known afresh to the
parish. But they need not have been anxious; a newsletter
circulated by the church a month before explaining why the
hoardings around All Souls were coming down and giving
warning of the visitation, prepared the way in many in-
stances. People expressed not only their appreciation of
being asked but also their intention of accepting the invitation. So Saturday 6 November was quite a day! Hundreds
of people poured through the front door from 11 a.m.
onwards, most of them strangers to any church, let alone All

107

Souls. Many of them agreed to attend a service in the future.

That Saturday had not been the only occasion when visitors had poured in, however. Wednesday lunch-time had been 'open house' for the staff in neighbouring banks, offices, shops and the BBC. From 7.30 a.m. that day, members of the congregation were out on the steps inviting people to call in at lunch-time. The result was an overwhelming flood of people in the space of a couple of hours, many rushing back to tell their colleagues to come and see . . . then returning themselves for a second look!

Sunday's services were so packed there was scarcely room to breathe – even with all the extra chairs and overflow facilities in use. But it was a privilege to see so many newcomers in the church and no service went by without some clear presentation of the good news of the gospel. New contacts and friendships were made afterwards in the relaxed atmosphere in the hall below.

Of course there were also teething problems. The lift broke down; the overhead projector screen refused to descend; the unusual chancel furniture was disliked by a few; the overflow facilities on Sunday mornings clashed with the Sunday school and there were complaints about the noise and lack of reverence in the church before the services. But, as Michael Baughen pleaded, so much of what was planned had worked: 'Let's be patient when things are not quite as we would wish.' Having got the ship safely launched, he explained, they were discovering that actually running it was a much bigger task than had been envisaged.

What was apparent in the first few months back in the new building was that the family had grown once again. All Souls was never less than full for every service, with many visitors who had come to listen or look. Some would no doubt eventually leave. Others would stay and become involved in the life of the church. There would not be room for many passengers – for it was – and is – a challenging, sometimes daunting, family to belong to, as many testify. With such men as John Stott and Michael Baughen in leadership, there is little time for complacency.

John Stott, whose dream of redeveloping All Souls had at last become reality, was well aware of the dangers of being a 'successful' church. He thanked God for the new building (even though his hope of radial seating throughout the ground floor had not come to full fruition!). He felt sure the congregation should be eternally grateful for Archdeacon Samuel Woodhouse's suggestion of the name of Robert Potter – 'whose great gift is to return to the beauty of a building's original architectural heritage – while adapting it to the needs of the modern world.'

John recognised readily that the greatest danger about All Souls was its size, acknowledging that this had always been the chief pastoral problem. 'Yet over against that there is a need for a strong evangelical centre in London. The fact that so many have given to the project from all over the country and the world, testifies, in my view, to their desire that All Souls should be preserved as such, for they feel they need this facility. But we do not want All Souls to be a "preaching centre", and I think we are more than that.'

He recognised, too, with sadness, that elsewhere, young people were voting with their feet and leaving the churches. He had spent some time analysing why. 'I believe they are looking for, and not finding, the following: a biblical contemporary preaching ministry which is faithful to Scripture and relevant to the modern world; a warm caring fellowship with authentic relationships of love within it; a church that takes outreach seriously to the local community; a worship which is a joyful celebration and bears witness to the reality of God in the midst; opportunities for lay people to exercise their God-given gifts in an every-member ministry . . . These are the five principles, under God, that we have always tried to develop at All Souls. I hope we will continue to do so now.'

For Michael Baughen the end of six years of intense and heavy responsibility for the building project had brought its own particular rewards. The new Waldegrave Hall was now the church family's lounge and was in full use as such. Easy chairs in clusters round low tables at the sides, gave it a relaxed feel. Coffee and hot meals were available from the refectory after most services and before many meetings. Many more people stayed to chat in comfort who would normally disappear home and miss out on the chance of fellowship. The acoustics of the new hall had also passed their test with flying colours, despite the well-muffled rumbling of the Victoria Line.

The other 'working wonder' which gave him great pleasure was the new reception desk, which had proved itself invaluable, helping all sorts of people with every type of problem and query. There was a real ministry in running this new facility. The welcome desk team of volunteers from the church family, who were specially briefed, was one way in which Michael's particular vision of a church into which people felt they could walk and feel welcome, had come true beyond his wildest dreams.

The visitor or enquirer who arrives at All Souls Church on a week-day evening will probably see the beautiful fluted cupola and pillared portico floodlit – a beacon of light at the top of Regent Street which John Nash himself might well have appreciated! As he comes nearer to the church he will find the front door open and, beyond the circular porch, he can see through glass doors the splendour and simplicity of the refurbished church. To the right is the Welcome Desk where there will always be someone to give help and guidance. Below, down the curving staircases to the basement, one or other of the church groups will probably be meeting in the hall.

'We see the restructured All Souls as a "lighted beacon" seven days a week,' stated the official Appeal Brochure, 'with its multiple evangelistic, teaching, training and caring activities at last centred on one building and not scattered around in other people's premises.' In God's goodness all this and more became a reality for the church of All Souls on 2 November 1976. It was little wonder that at the Re-dedication Service, with full hearts, the church family sang to the tune 'Londonderry Air' these words specially written for the occasion by Michael Baughen:

1 We could not tell how you would take us forward, Lord,
   To do your will and see your plan fulfilled.
   We came in prayer to seek your inspiration
   To lead us on, we knew not how or when.
   And now this day we bring you praise and glory
   For you alone have brought us to this time,
   In your great power you took away all barriers.
   Great is your faithfulness – All honour to your name!

2 We could not tell how we would find resources, Lord,
   To see us through a work so large and long
   But, as we prayed, and sought your all-sufficiency
   We saw your word and promises proved true.
   And now this day we bring you praise and glory
   For you have done more than we asked or thought:
   You opened wide the windows of your heaven
   And poured out blessing to the honour of your name.

3 We could not tell how you would bring enrichment, Lord,
   To hearts and lives renewed with faith in you,
   But as we prayed your Spirit moved upon us all
   And opened hearts in deepened love and joy.
   And now this day we bring you praise and glory
   For every token of your gracious love.
   You are our God, the God of the impossible
   And we rejoice to see the honour of your name!

4 We cannot tell all you have planned and purposed, Lord,
   To use this church renewed to spread your word,
   And so we pray that we may be obedient
   To do your will whatever that may be.
   And now this day, as we bring praise and glory
   We bring our lives in sacrificial love –
   Take us, O Lord, and use us for your kingdom
   As church and people help us glorify your name!